Norwegian Fjords Cruise
Travel Guide 2025

A Traveler's Guide to Norway's Most Breathtaking Cruising Routes, Scenic Ports, and Authentic Cultural Encounters

Harry J. Wealth

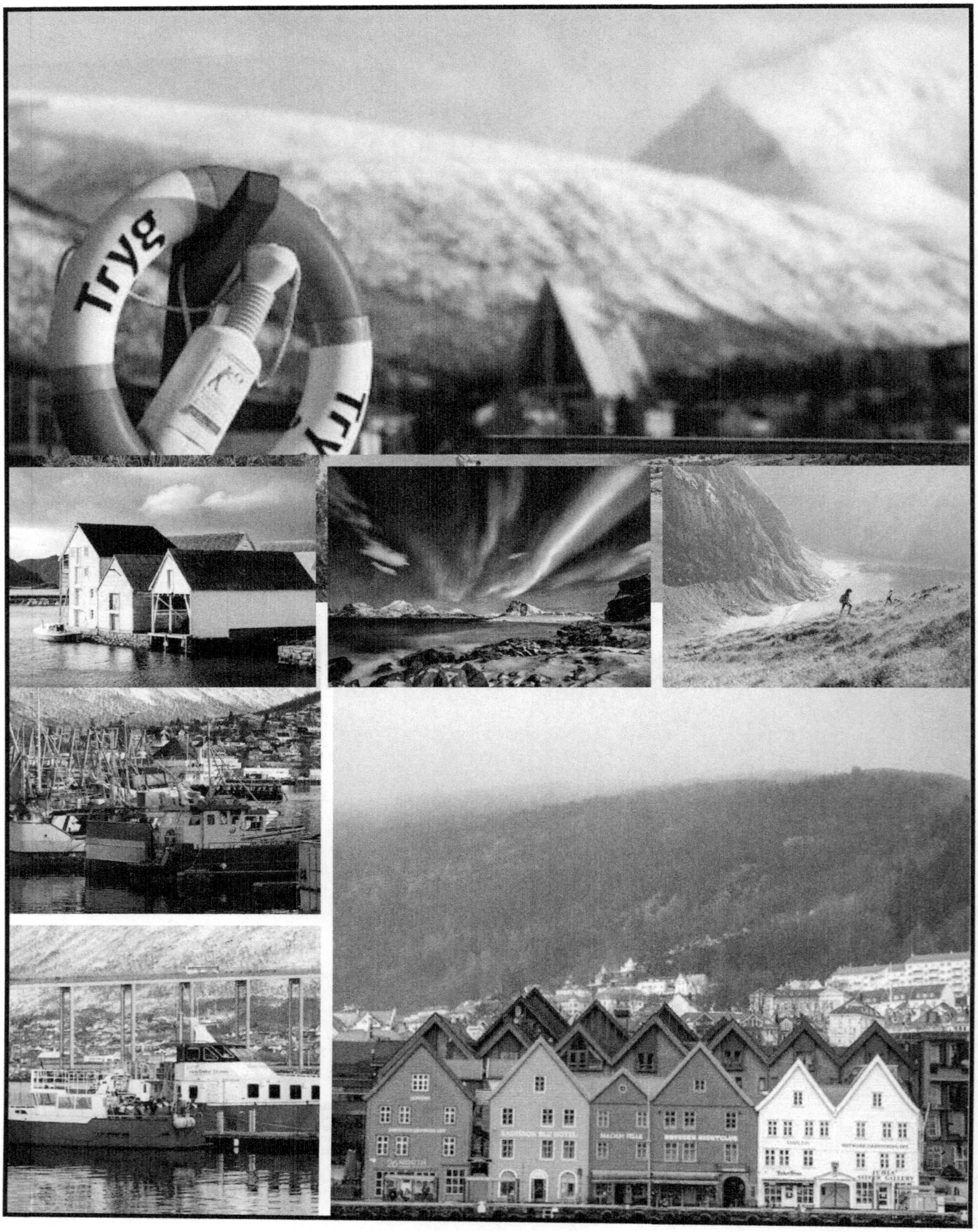
Tryg

Copyright © 2025, Harry J. Wealth

All rights reserved. No part of this travel guide may be reproduced, distributed, or transmitted in any form or by any means, including photocopying, recording, or other electronic or mechanical methods, without the prior written permission of the publisher, except in the case of brief quotations embodied in critical reviews and cert... write to the publisher

Disclaimer

While every effort has been made to ensure the accuracy of the information contained in this guide, the author and publisher assume no responsibility for errors, omissions, or changes in details. The information provided is for general informational purposes only and should not be considered as professional advice. Travelers are encouraged to verify all details with the relevant authorities and service providers before making any travel arrangements.

Table Of Content

Chapter 1: Welcome to the Fjords — 6
    Understanding the allure of the Norwegian Fjords — 6
    The unique blend of natural beauty, history, and adventure — 9
    Why cruising is the ideal way to explore — 11

Chapter 2: Choosing Your Perfect Cruise — 15
    Top cruise lines offering Norwegian Fjord itineraries — 15
    Small ships vs. large ships: Pros and cons — 18
    Tailoring your experience: Luxury, family-friendly, and budget options — 21

Chapter 3: Timing Your Adventure — 25
    Seasons in the Fjords — 25
    Month-by-month breakdown of what to expect — 28
    Weather, wildlife, and cultural highlights — 31

Chapter 4: Packing Essentials — 35
    The ultimate packing list for all seasons — 35
    Dressing for unpredictable weather in the Fjords — 38
    Must-have accessories for hiking, photography, and cruise life — 40

Chapter 5: Iconic Fjords and Stunning Landscapes — 44
    Geirangerfjord: The breathtaking jewel — 44
    Nærøyfjord: UNESCO-protected beauty — 46
    Hardangerfjord: The orchard of Norway — 49
    Sognefjord: The king of fjords — 52

Chapter 6: Ports of Call — 56
    Bergen: The cultural heart of the Fjords — 56
    Ålesund: Art Nouveau architecture and adventure — 59
    Stavanger: A mix of history and nature — 62
    Tromsø: The Arctic capital — 65

Chapter 7: Shore Excursions and Activities — 69
    Hiking the trails of Norwegian legends — 69
    Kayaking through serene fjord waters — 72
    Unique wildlife encounters: Puffins, whales, and more — 74
    Experiencing farm visits and local life in fjord-side villages — 77

Chapter 8: Culinary Adventures — 81
    Traditional Norwegian flavors: From fresh seafood to reindeer — 81
    Best local dishes to try at each port — 84

Café culture and must-visit restaurants	86
Crafting the perfect onboard dining experience	89
Chapter 9: ACCOMMODATION	**92**
Luxury Hotels: Where to experience opulence and panoramic fjord views.	92
Mid-Range and Budget Hotels: Comfortable stays for every traveler.	95
Cabins and Cottages: Cozy retreats close to nature.	97
Farm Stays: Immersive rural experiences with local charm.	100
Cruise Ship Cabins: Uninterrupted Fjord Views from the Water	103
Airbnb and Vacation Rentals: Unique and Flexible Options for Personalized Stays	104
Chapter 10: Sustainability and Responsible Travel	**107**
Reducing your environmental impact as a traveler	107
Supporting local communities and economies	110
Chapter 11: Practical Travel Tips	**114**
Navigating Norwegian culture and etiquette	114
Currency and language basics	116
Emergency contacts and safety tips	118
Chapter 12: The Journey's End	**121**
Conclusion: A Journey Worth Taking	121

Chapter 1: Welcome to the Fjords

Understanding the allure of the Norwegian Fjords

Imagine a place where towering cliffs plunge dramatically into still, glassy waters; where cascading waterfalls braid through emerald forests; and where the air feels fresher, cleaner, and imbued with the timeless rhythm of nature itself. This is the world of the Norwegian Fjords—a landscape so majestic and so unique that it has captivated travelers, artists, and adventurers for centuries. To stand in their presence is to witness the Earth's artistry at its finest.

But what is it about the Norwegian Fjords that continues to allure visitors from across the globe? Let me guide you through their mystique, their raw beauty, and the deeper connection they inspire.

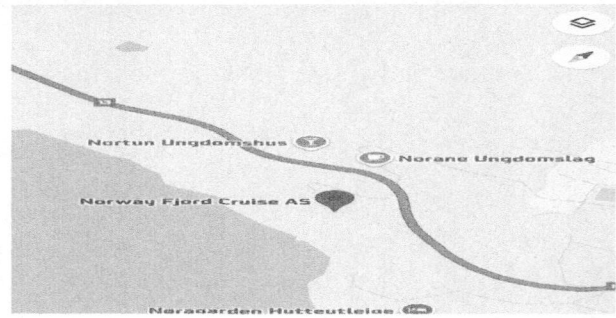

The Dramatic Geography: Nature's Handiwork

The fjords were carved during the Ice Ages, as enormous glaciers retreated, leaving behind these deep, narrow waterways flanked by steep cliffs. These natural formations are marvels of both geology and artistry, an eternal reminder of nature's power and creativity.

What Makes Them Unique

Sheer Depth and Scale:
Some fjords, like Sognefjord (known as the "King of the Fjords"), stretch over 200 kilometers inland, plunging to depths of nearly 1,300 meters. These dimensions create an imposing and otherworldly atmosphere that feels almost humbling.

Endless Waterfalls:
As you traverse the fjords, waterfalls seem to spill from every cliff. Geirangerfjord, for instance, boasts the famous Seven Sisters waterfall, where seven distinct streams descend in unison like ribbons unfurling in the wind.

My Observation:
On my first trip to Nærøyfjord, I was struck by how the stillness of the water mirrored the sheer cliffs so perfectly. Each ripple in the reflection felt like it was whispering secrets of the ages, and every narrow passage felt like being cradled by the Earth itself.

A Symphony of Seasons
The Norwegian Fjords transform with the seasons, and each period offers its own kind of enchantment.

Spring and Summer: The Vibrant Fjords
What to Expect:
During the warmer months, the fjords burst into life. Orchards bloom in Hardangerfjord, and the midnight sun casts a golden glow over serene landscapes.

Why It's Special:
Kayaking in the glassy waters or hiking trails that hug the fjordside feels like an intimate conversation with nature. Wildlife—whales, seals, and eagles—come alive during this period, adding an extra dimension of wonder.

Autumn: A Tapestry of Colors
What to Expect:
The forests surrounding the fjords turn into a sea of fiery reds, oranges, and yellows. The crispness in the air adds an invigorating quality to any outdoor adventure.

Winter: The Magical Fjords
What to Expect:
In winter, the fjords become a quieter, more introspective destination. Frozen waterfalls and snow-draped cliffs create a landscape straight out of a fairytale. For many, this is the best time to chase the ethereal Northern Lights dancing above.

My Experience:
I remember gazing out at Tromsø's fjord in winter, where the silent white landscape was suddenly illuminated by the green and purple hues of the aurora. It felt otherworldly, as though the sky itself were alive.

Unmatched Tranquility
There is something deeply meditative about the fjords. The stillness of the water, the distant sound of cascading waterfalls, and the whispering wind all create a serene atmosphere. In this space, time feels irrelevant, and the rush of modern life falls away.

What to Observe
The Silence:
Often, the loudest thing you'll hear is the sound of your own breath. This silence is so rare in our modern world that it feels almost like a gift.

The Sky and Water Connection:
The fjords blur the line between earth and sky. Clouds seem to drift across the water, and

reflections create a doubled world that feels ethereal.

Cultural and Historical Richness

The fjords are not just geographical wonders—they are steeped in history and lore. They were the lifeblood of the Viking Age, serving as trading routes and offering protection to settlements. Even today, the quaint villages along the fjords remain bastions of Norwegian heritage.

The Viking Legacy
Visiting Viking museums along the fjords provides a deep dive into the culture of these fearless seafarers. Towns like Gudvangen host immersive Viking experiences, complete with reconstructed longhouses and authentic Viking ships.

Fjordside Villages
Villages like Flåm, Ålesund, and Eidfjord reflect the charm of traditional Norwegian life, from colorful wooden houses to bustling local markets.
My Experience:
In Flåm, I struck up a conversation with a local shopkeeper who shared how her family had fished the fjords for generations. Her stories added a layer of humanity to the landscape, reminding me that these majestic fjords are also home to vibrant, enduring communities.

<u>Nature's Playground: Endless Adventures</u>
For outdoor enthusiasts, the fjords are a wonderland of activity.
Hiking
The Preikestolen (Pulpit Rock) hike above Lysefjord is a bucket-list experience, offering a dizzying view of the fjord below.
Personal Moment:
Reaching the top, where the massive rock juts out over the abyss, I remember the way my heart raced—not from exertion, but from the sheer thrill of standing at such a vertigo-inducing edge.

Water Activities
- Kayaking across the still fjord waters brings you closer to nature in a way few other experiences can. You can glide past cascading waterfalls, explore hidden coves, and see seals basking on rocks.
- Cruises, whether small ship or larger vessel, are also a fantastic way to take in the fjords' vastness.

Wildlife Watching
The fjords are home to an array of wildlife. Spotting humpback whales breaking the water's surface or white-tailed eagles soaring overhead is nothing short of magical.

A Journey of Self-Reflection

Above all, the allure of the Norwegian Fjords lies in the way they make you feel. To be among their grandeur is to feel humbled, connected, and inspired. It's a reminder that the world is vast and full of wonder, and that we are only small pieces in an awe-inspiring puzzle.

What I Experienced:
There was a moment, sitting on a rock by Geirangerfjord, when I felt completely at

peace. The sun was low, the air crisp, and the fjord's surface utterly still. It was as though the world had paused just for me—a pause that felt less like an end and more like a beginning.

The unique blend of natural beauty, history, and adventure

Few places on Earth can claim to be as richly layered as the Norwegian Fjords—a region where nature, history, and adventure come together in a breathtaking symphony. These fjords are more than just a destination; they are a world unto themselves, brimming with contrasts and connections that speak to every traveler's heart. From cliffs that echo the whispers of history to waterways that invite thrilling exploration, the Norwegian Fjords offer an experience that is truly one of a kind.

A Landscape of Awe: The Natural Beauty of the Fjords

The beauty of the Norwegian Fjords lies in their raw, untamed majesty—a combination of towering cliffs, glassy waters, and vibrant ecosystems. These landscapes feel alive, constantly shifting with the light, the seasons, and even the time of day.

Iconic Natural Wonders

Geirangerfjord:
This UNESCO World Heritage Site is often regarded as the most beautiful fjord in the world, with its narrow waterway flanked by sheer cliffs, dotted with cascading waterfalls like the Seven Sisters and the Suitor.
My Experience: Standing on the deck of a ship as it glided into Geirangerfjord, I was struck by the sheer drama of the cliffs rising on either side. I watched as sunlight glinted off the waterfalls, creating rainbows that danced across the mist. In that moment, I felt as though I had stepped into a fairytale.

Hardangerfjord:
Known as the "Orchard of Norway," this fjord offers a softer beauty, with apple and cherry blossoms in spring giving way to orchards laden with fruit in summer.
What to Observe: In May, the fjordside blossoms create a scene of pastoral perfection, contrasting vividly with the snow-capped peaks above.

Nærøyfjord:
This narrow, almost otherworldly fjord is another UNESCO World Heritage Site. Its tranquil waters reflect the cliffs so perfectly that it creates the illusion of a doubled world.

The Seasonal Magic

Every season transforms the fjords into something new and enchanting. In the summer, the long days of the Midnight Sun drape the landscapes in golden light, while autumn's fiery hues bring a sense of coziness and reflection. Winter, meanwhile, is a crystalline wonderland of frozen waterfalls and snow-blanketed cliffs—a perfect setting for the ethereal Northern Lights.

Echoes of the Past: The Historical Richness of the Fjords

The fjords are more than geographical wonders—they are the keepers of history, from the seafaring Vikings to the quaint villages that have thrived along their shores for generations. Exploring these regions is like stepping into a living timeline, where ancient tales and modern life intertwine seamlessly.

The Viking Legacy

The Norwegian Fjords were the lifeblood of the Viking Age, providing both protection and passage for these legendary seafarers. To sail the fjords is to follow in the wake of Viking ships that once explored the far reaches of the world.

Gudvangen:

This small village on the edge of the Nærøyfjord is known as the Viking Valley, a living museum where you can immerse yourself in the Viking way of life.

What to Do: Watch blacksmiths at work, feast on traditional Viking fare, and explore reconstructed longhouses.

What I Felt: Walking among reenactors dressed in period clothing made me feel as though the centuries had folded in on themselves. Listening to a storyteller recount Viking myths as the fjord's still waters reflected the mountains felt deeply grounding.

Historic Villages
Bergen:

Often called the "Gateway to the Fjords," Bergen is a city steeped in history, from its vibrant Hanseatic Wharf (Bryggen) to its centuries-old fish markets. Wandering its cobblestone streets is a journey through time.

Ålesund:

This port city, rebuilt in stunning Art Nouveau style after a fire in 1904, blends history and beauty. Climbing Mount Aksla offers panoramic views that reveal how deeply the city is intertwined with the fjords.

Living Traditions

The people of the fjords have nurtured traditions for generations. Whether it's the crafting of wooden boats or the singing of old folk songs, these customs keep history alive in the most beautiful way.

An Adventurer's Paradise: The Fjords in Action

The Norwegian Fjords invite not just admiration but participation. From hiking the cliffs to kayaking the waters, the fjords are a playground for those seeking connection through adventure.

Hiking the Fjords
Preikestolen (Pulpit Rock):

This iconic cliff above Lysefjord offers one of the most dramatic views in the world. The 4-hour round-trip hike is worth every step, with the sight of the cliff's flat top jutting out over the void creating equal parts awe and exhilaration.

What I Observed: Reaching the summit, I saw hikers celebrating together, a mix of languages and cultures united by a shared sense of accomplishment. Watching the fjord stretch endlessly below, I felt the kind of joy that only comes from earning a view.

Romsdalseggen Ridge:

This lesser-known but equally stunning hike offers panoramic views of both the fjords and the surrounding valleys. It's a quieter alternative for those seeking solitude in nature.

Exploring the Waterways
Kayaking:
Gliding through the fjords in a kayak brings an intimacy to the experience. You'll find yourself eye-level with seals, passing beneath waterfalls, and discovering hidden coves that larger vessels cannot reach.
My Experience: Paddling through Nærøyfjord early in the morning, I was enveloped in silence save for the sound of my paddle dipping into the water. It was as though the fjord itself were holding its breath.

Cruising:
Whether you choose a large cruise ship or a smaller, more intimate vessel, cruising allows you to witness the fjords' vastness in comfort. On deck, with the wind in your hair and the cliffs towering around you, the sense of adventure is palpable.

Winter Adventures
Dog Sledding and Snowshoeing:
In the colder months, the fjords transform into an Arctic playground. Imagine the thrill of being pulled by huskies across snowy landscapes or trekking through silent forests with snow crunching beneath your feet.

Why cruising is the ideal way to explore

The Norwegian Fjords are not just a destination—they are an experience, a journey through landscapes so majestic they defy the imagination. But with such a vast and intricate region to discover, the question arises: what is the best way to explore it? Enter cruising—a mode of travel that not only offers unparalleled convenience but also places you right in the heart of these spectacular waterways. Whether you're a first-time visitor or a seasoned explorer, cruising unlocks the wonders of the fjords in ways no other form of travel can.

Effortless Access to Remote Beauty
The Norwegian Fjords are a network of long, narrow inlets that stretch deep into the countryside, surrounded by towering cliffs and often accessible only by water. Cruising offers the rare privilege of reaching these remote areas effortlessly.

Advantages
No Need for Overland Travel:
Roads in the fjord regions are often winding and require lengthy detours. A cruise ship glides directly into these natural havens, saving you time and offering an uninterrupted journey.
Up-Close Views:
From the deck of a ship, you can watch waterfalls cascade down cliffs, spot seals basking on rocks, and marvel at the sheer scale of the fjords.

What I Observed:
Sailing into Geirangerfjord, the cliffs felt so close I could almost reach out and touch them. Waterfalls like the Seven Sisters streamed down in silvery ribbons, and the stillness of the water created perfect reflections. It was as though the fjord was embracing the ship, allowing us to become part of its majesty.

Comfort Without Compromise

One of the most compelling reasons to choose a cruise is the comfort it provides. The Norwegian Fjords offer rugged, untamed beauty, but you don't have to sacrifice modern amenities to enjoy them.

Advantages
Luxury at Sea:
Cruise ships are essentially floating hotels, offering comfortable cabins, gourmet dining, and even spas—all while transporting you to some of the most remote corners of the world.
Variety of Accommodations:
From budget-friendly interior cabins to luxurious suites with private balconies, there's an option for every traveler.
Price Range: Cruises for the Norwegian Fjords typically start at €1,000 per person for a 7-day itinerary, but costs vary based on the ship and cabin type.

What I Experienced:
After a long day of exploring the charming village of Flåm, I returned to the ship and soaked in a hot tub on the upper deck, sipping wine as the sun set over the fjord. It was the perfect blend of adventure and relaxation—a balance that's hard to achieve with overland travel alone.

A Front-Row Seat to Ever-Changing Scenery
On a cruise, the journey is just as captivating as the destinations. The fjords are landscapes of perpetual motion, with shifting light, misty mornings, and golden sunsets creating an ever-changing panorama.

Advantages
Non-Stop Views:
Unlike traveling by car or train, a cruise allows you to be surrounded by the fjords 24/7. Even while dining, relaxing, or sleeping, you remain immersed in the scenery.
Prime Positioning:
Many cruise itineraries are carefully timed to ensure you enter iconic fjords like Geiranger or Nærøyfjord during the most photogenic parts of the day.

What to Observe:
Watch how the fjords transform with the weather—sunlight playing off cliffs, mist rolling in from the water, or rain creating countless tiny waterfalls. These moments are fleeting but unforgettable.

A Variety of Destinations Without the Hassle
Cruising allows you to explore multiple destinations in a single trip, without the need

to repack your bags or navigate between towns.

Key Ports of Call
Bergen:
Known as the "Gateway to the Fjords," this vibrant city offers the historic Bryggen Wharf, bustling fish markets, and the chance to ascend Mount Fløyen for sweeping views.
Ålesund:
This Art Nouveau town is not only visually stunning but also serves as a gateway to nearby fjords and islands.
Stavanger:
From here, you can hike to Preikestolen (Pulpit Rock), one of Norway's most iconic landmarks.
Flåm:
Famous for the Flåm Railway, this village is a jumping-off point for adventures in the surrounding mountains and valleys.

Effortless Travel Between Ports
Each morning, you wake up in a new destination, ready to explore. No need to navigate roads, unpack at a new hotel, or worry about logistics—it's all taken care of.

Opportunities for Adventure and Exploration
Cruising doesn't mean you're confined to the ship—quite the opposite. Shore excursions offer a wide range of activities, from gentle sightseeing to adrenaline-pumping adventures.

Popular Excursions
Hiking and Nature Walks:
Explore trails that lead to waterfalls, panoramic viewpoints, and quaint fjordside villages. Many excursions cater to all fitness levels, ensuring everyone can participate.
Example: A guided hike to Vøringsfossen waterfall costs around €60–€90.
Kayaking:
Paddle through the serene waters of the fjords for a closer look at their cliffs, caves, and wildlife.
Example: Kayak tours in Geirangerfjord start at €70 per person.
Cultural Experiences:
Visit Viking museums, learn about local traditions, or attend a Norwegian folk music performance.

What I Experienced:
During a shore excursion in Tromsø, I joined a Sami guide for a reindeer-sledding experience. As the sled glided across the snow-covered fjord, the guide shared stories of his culture and his connection to the land. It was an adventure that extended beyond the physical and became deeply personal.

A Sustainable Choice
Modern cruise lines are increasingly focused on minimizing their environmental impact, making cruising a more sustainable way to explore the fjords.

Eco-Friendly Practices
Smaller, More Efficient Ships:
Many lines use smaller vessels specifically designed for the fjords, reducing emissions and impact on the waterways.
Partnerships with Local Communities:
Cruise lines often collaborate with local businesses, ensuring that tourism directly benefits the fjordside towns and villages.

What to Look For: Choose cruise lines certified by sustainable tourism organizations, such as Hurtigruten.

Catering to Every Type of Traveler
Cruising offers something for everyone, whether you're an adventurer, a foodie, or someone seeking peace and quiet.

For Families
Onboard activities like pools, kid-friendly entertainment, and child-focused excursions ensure a memorable trip for the whole family.

For Solo Travelers
Organized group excursions provide opportunities to meet like-minded travelers.

For Couples
Private balcony cabins and intimate dining experiences make cruises a romantic way to explore the fjords.

Final Thoughts
there's something undeniably magical about exploring the Norwegian Fjords by cruise. It's more than just a mode of travel—it's a seamless blend of comfort, adventure, and immersion. From the moment your ship glides into a fjord, you'll understand why this is the ideal way to experience these landscapes. The fjords are as vast as they are intricate, and cruising ensures you don't just visit them—you truly live them.

Chapter 2: Choosing Your Perfect Cruise

Top cruise lines offering Norwegian Fjord itineraries

Embarking on a cruise through the Norwegian Fjords is like stepping into a world where nature's grandeur meets tranquility. The towering cliffs, cascading waterfalls, and serene waters of the fjords create an unparalleled backdrop for exploration. But with so many cruise lines offering itineraries in this breathtaking region, how do you choose the one that's right for you? Let me guide you through the top cruise lines that specialize in Norwegian Fjord itineraries, each offering unique experiences tailored to different types of travelers.

1. Hurtigruten: The Authentic Norwegian Experience
Why Choose Hurtigruten?

Hurtigruten is often referred to as the "Coastal Express" and is deeply rooted in Norwegian culture. Operating since 1893, this line offers an authentic and immersive experience, focusing on connecting travelers with the local communities and landscapes.

Key Features
- Small Ships: Hurtigruten's smaller vessels allow access to remote fjords and villages that larger ships cannot reach.
- Sustainability: The line is a pioneer in eco-friendly cruising, with hybrid-powered ships like the MS Roald Amundsen and MS Fridtjof Nansen.

- **Local Cuisine:** Onboard dining features locally sourced ingredients, offering a true taste of Norway.

Itineraries
- **Classic Coastal Voyage:** A 12-day round trip from Bergen to Kirkenes, stopping at 34 ports along the way.
- **Northern Lights Cruises:** Winter itineraries designed to maximize your chances of seeing the aurora borealis.

What I Observed
Sailing with Hurtigruten felt like stepping into the rhythm of Norwegian life. At each port, locals greeted the ship as though welcoming old friends. The onboard lectures about Viking history and Arctic wildlife added depth to the journey, making it as educational as it was awe-inspiring.

2. Viking Ocean Cruises: Luxury Meets Exploration

Why Choose Viking?
Viking Ocean Cruises is synonymous with understated luxury and cultural enrichment. Their Norwegian Fjord itineraries are designed for travelers who want to explore in style while delving into the region's history and culture.

Key Features
- **Elegant Ships:** Viking's small to mid-sized ships offer spacious staterooms, infinity pools, and Scandinavian-inspired design.
- **Cultural Focus:** Onboard enrichment programs include lectures, cooking classes, and performances inspired by Norwegian traditions.
- **Inclusive Pricing:** Fares include shore excursions, Wi-Fi, and specialty dining, ensuring a seamless experience.

Itineraries
- **Viking Shores & Fjords:** A 7-night journey from Bergen to Amsterdam, visiting iconic fjords like Geirangerfjord and Hardangerfjord.
- **Into the Midnight Sun:** A 14-night cruise from Bergen to London, exploring the Arctic Circle and the Lofoten Islands.

What I Observed
The attention to detail on Viking cruises is unparalleled. From the heated bathroom floors in my stateroom to the curated shore excursions, every aspect of the journey felt thoughtfully designed. Watching the Midnight Sun from the ship's infinity pool was a moment of pure magic.

3. Norwegian Cruise Line (NCL): Adventure and Accessibility

Why Choose NCL?
Norwegian Cruise Line is perfect for travelers seeking a mix of adventure, entertainment, and flexibility. Their larger ships cater to families and groups, offering a wide range of activities both onboard and ashore.

Key Features
- **Freestyle Cruising:** No fixed dining times or dress codes, allowing for a more relaxed experience.

- **Family-Friendly:** Onboard activities include water parks, Broadway-style shows, and kids' clubs.
- **Diverse Excursions:** Options range from hiking and kayaking to cultural tours.

Itineraries
- **Norwegian Fjords Cruise:** A 7-night round trip from Southampton, visiting Stavanger, Bergen, and Geirangerfjord.
- **Northern Europe & Fjords:** A 12-night itinerary combining the fjords with stops in Iceland and the British Isles.

What I Observed
NCL's ships are like floating resorts, offering something for everyone. After a day of hiking to Pulpit Rock, I returned to the ship for a lively evening show and a delicious meal at one of the specialty restaurants. The balance of adventure and relaxation was perfect.

4. Holland America Line: Classic Elegance
Why Choose Holland America?
Holland America Line is known for its timeless elegance and focus on destination immersion. Their Norwegian Fjord cruises cater to travelers who appreciate a refined atmosphere and in-depth exploration.

Key Features
- **Mid-Sized Ships:** Spacious yet intimate, with fewer passengers than mega-ships.
- **Enrichment Programs:** Onboard activities include cooking demonstrations, photography workshops, and lectures about Norwegian culture.
- **Exceptional Dining:** The Pinnacle Grill and other specialty restaurants offer gourmet cuisine inspired by the destinations.

Itineraries
- **Norwegian Fjords Explorer:** A 7-night cruise from Rotterdam, visiting Eidfjord, Bergen, and Geirangerfjord.
- **Northern Isles:** A 14-night journey combining the fjords with stops in Scotland and Iceland.

What I Observed
Holland America's ships exude a sense of calm sophistication. I spent hours on the observation deck, watching the fjords unfold like a living painting. The onboard naturalist's commentary added layers of meaning to the scenery, making the experience deeply enriching.

5. Celebrity Cruises: Modern Luxury
Why Choose Celebrity?
Celebrity Cruises offers a contemporary take on luxury, with sleek ships, innovative dining, and a focus on wellness. Their Norwegian Fjord itineraries are ideal for travelers who want a stylish and rejuvenating experience.

Key Features
- **Innovative Design:** Ships feature unique spaces like the Magic Carpet, a cantilevered platform that offers stunning views.
- **Wellness Focus:** The onboard spa and fitness programs are perfect for travelers seeking relaxation and rejuvenation.

- Culinary Excellence: Michelin-starred chefs curate the menus, ensuring every meal is a delight.

Itineraries
- Scandinavia & Fjords: A 9-night cruise from Amsterdam, visiting Oslo, Bergen, and Stavanger.
- Arctic Circle Adventure: A 12-night journey exploring the fjords and the northern reaches of Norway.

What I Observed
Celebrity's ships feel like boutique hotels at sea. After a day of kayaking in Nærøyfjord, I indulged in a massage at the spa and dined on fresh seafood paired with fine wine. The combination of adventure and luxury was unforgettable.

6. Princess Cruises: A Balanced Experience
Why Choose Princess?
Princess Cruises strikes a balance between adventure and comfort, offering itineraries that highlight the best of the Norwegian Fjords while providing a relaxing onboard experience.

Key Features
- MedallionClass Technology: Personalized service and seamless navigation of the ship.
- Destination-Focused Dining: Regional specialties are featured in the menus, bringing the flavors of Norway onboard.
- Variety of Activities: From enrichment lectures to live entertainment, there's something for everyone.

Itineraries
Norwegian Fjords: A 7-night cruise from Southampton, visiting Stavanger, Olden, and Bergen.
Land of the Midnight Sun: A 14-night journey exploring the Arctic Circle and the Lofoten Islands.

What I Observed
Princess Cruises offers a sense of ease and balance. I loved starting my mornings with yoga on the deck, followed by excursions to explore fjordside villages. Evenings were spent enjoying live music and stargazing from the top deck.

Small ships vs. large ships: Pros and cons

Choosing the right ship for your Norwegian Fjords adventure is one of the most important decisions you'll make when planning your cruise. The type of ship you select—small or large—can shape every aspect of your experience, from the places you visit to the way you feel while exploring this breathtaking region. Each option has its unique advantages and challenges, and understanding the differences will ensure you select the one that's perfect for your travel style and priorities.

Small Ships: Intimate and Immersive

Small ships, ranging from boutique expedition vessels to luxury yachts, usually accommodate fewer than 300 passengers. These ships are designed for travelers who value intimate experiences and a deeper connection to nature and local culture.

Pros of Small Ships

1. Access to Remote Fjords and Smaller Ports
Small ships have the agility to navigate narrow fjords and access secluded areas that larger ships cannot reach. Fjords like Nærøyfjord, one of the narrowest in Norway, are best explored on smaller vessels.
Example: Many small ships can dock directly in charming villages like Flåm or Gudvangen, whereas larger ships may have to use tender boats or dock farther away.
What I Observed: Cruising into Nærøyfjord on a small ship felt like entering another world. The steep cliffs loomed close, and the silence was punctuated only by waterfalls cascading into the fjord. It was an intimate encounter with nature that felt impossibly personal.

2. Fewer Crowds and a Personalized Experience
With fewer passengers, small ships foster a sense of camaraderie and community. You're more likely to interact with the crew, naturalists, and fellow travelers.
Dining is often less hectic, and shore excursions can be more tailored to your interests. Imagine disembarking with just a handful of fellow adventurers instead of hundreds!
What I Felt: On a small ship, the captain often joined us for dinner, sharing stories about navigating the fjords and offering tips for the best wildlife-spotting opportunities. It felt like being part of an exclusive, close-knit expedition.

3. Deeper Cultural and Educational Enrichment
Small ships often focus on providing meaningful experiences. Think in-depth shore excursions, onboard lectures, and guided nature walks with experts who help you connect with the history, geology, and ecosystems of the fjords.
Hurtigruten and other boutique lines emphasize sustainable tourism and invite local experts onboard to share their knowledge.

4. Eco-Friendly and Sustainable
Many small ships are eco-conscious, designed to leave minimal impact on the fragile fjord ecosystems. Hybrid-powered and renewable energy options are often featured.

Cons of Small Ships
1. Higher Cost
Smaller ships often come with a premium price tag, reflecting the exclusivity and personalized experiences they offer.
Typical Costs: Cruises on small ships can start at €3,000–€5,000 per person for a 7-day itinerary.

2. Limited Amenities
While small ships offer cozy lounges and fine dining, they typically lack the variety of

facilities found on larger ships, such as theaters, multiple restaurants, or extensive spas.

3. Fewer Onboard Activities
Small ships prioritize exploration and enrichment over onboard entertainment, which may not suit families or travelers seeking constant activity.

Large Ships: Comfort and Variety
Large ships, like those operated by Norwegian Cruise Line (NCL), Celebrity Cruises, or Princess Cruises, accommodate anywhere from 1,500 to over 5,000 passengers. These vessels are floating cities, offering countless amenities and diverse experiences.

Pros of Large Ships
1. Extensive Onboard Amenities
- Large ships are packed with activities, from swimming pools and water parks to theaters, casinos, and spas.
- Dining options are vast, with everything from casual buffets to fine-dining restaurants featuring globally inspired menus.

2. Family-Friendly Features
- Large ships cater to families with kids' clubs, water slides, climbing walls, and even arcades.
- Multigenerational families can find something for everyone, making these ships ideal for group travel.

What I Observed: Watching children race down water slides while their parents enjoyed a relaxing soak in the pool was a reminder that large ships make family travel effortless and fun.

3. Affordable Options
Large ships benefit from economies of scale, making their cruises more accessible to budget-conscious travelers.
Typical Costs: Norwegian Fjord itineraries on large ships can start as low as €1,000–€1,500 per person for a 7-day trip, depending on the cabin type.

4. Diverse Entertainment and Dining
- Broadway-style shows, live music, and themed events ensure there's never a dull moment onboard.
- Culinary options cater to every palate, whether you're craving sushi, steak, or Norwegian-inspired dishes.

5. Smooth Sailing Experience
Larger ships are more stable, which can reduce the chance of seasickness—a key advantage for first-time cruisers.

Cons of Large Ships
1. Limited Access to Small Fjords
- Due to their size, large ships are restricted to wider fjords and may not be able to enter narrow passages like Nærøyfjord.
- Larger ships often anchor offshore, requiring passengers to take tender boats to smaller ports.

2. Crowds
With thousands of passengers onboard, public spaces can feel crowded, especially during peak dining hours or when disembarking for excursions.
What I Observed: Boarding tenders with hundreds of other passengers can detract from

the serenity of the fjords, particularly when everyone is eager to get ashore.

3. Less Personalized
While large ships offer plenty of activities, their sheer size can make the experience feel less intimate. Interactions with the crew and guides are often less personal.

4. Environmental Impact
Larger ships tend to have a higher environmental footprint, though many cruise lines are taking steps to reduce emissions and promote sustainability.

Choosing the Right Ship for You
Ultimately, the choice between a small and large ship depends on your travel preferences, priorities, and budget.

Small Ships Are Ideal If You:
- Want an intimate, immersive experience that prioritizes nature and culture.
- Are willing to pay a premium for exclusive destinations and personalized service.
- Value quiet moments and smaller groups.

Large Ships Are Perfect If You:
Seek variety in onboard entertainment and dining.
Are traveling with a family or larger group.
Want a more affordable option without sacrificing comfort.

Tailoring your experience: Luxury, family-friendly, and budget options

Embarking on a Norwegian Fjords cruise is like stepping into a world where nature and serenity reign supreme. The fjords are a destination for everyone—whether you're seeking lavish indulgence, meaningful family adventures, or an unforgettable trip on a budget. The secret lies in tailoring your experience to suit your preferences, travel companions, and budget.

Luxury: Experiencing the Fjords in Opulence

If your dream fjord cruise involves unparalleled comfort, exclusive access to secluded areas, and exceptional service, luxury cruising is the way to go. Luxury cruises are designed to elevate every moment, ensuring that your journey is as extraordinary as the destinations themselves.

Features of Luxury Cruises
1. Boutique Ships and Suites
Luxury cruise lines like Viking Ocean Cruises, Seabourn, and Silversea offer elegant, mid-sized vessels with spacious suites. Many suites feature private balconies, allowing you

to wake up to views of cascading waterfalls and jagged cliffs without leaving your room.
Price Range: Starting from €5,000 per person for a 7-night cruise, depending on the suite and itinerary.

2. Personalized Service
Butler service, concierge assistance, and a high crew-to-guest ratio ensure your every need is met.
What I Observed: On a luxury fjord cruise, I was greeted by name from the moment I stepped on board. My butler arranged private excursions and brought me a tailored picnic basket for a hike along the fjord—an intimate touch that elevated the whole experience.

3. Gourmet Dining
Michelin-starred chefs design menus inspired by local Norwegian ingredients, such as Arctic char and cloudberries. Specialty dining venues create culinary masterpieces that reflect the fjords' flavors.

4. Exclusive Excursions
Smaller luxury ships can access remote fjords and organize private excursions, such as kayaking in Nærøyfjord or dining with a local family in their fjordside village.
Example: A helicopter tour over Lysefjord or private yacht charters for intimate fjord exploration (€1,000+ per excursion).

Why Choose Luxury?
For moments of profound tranquility, like soaking in a private hot tub on your balcony as the Midnight Sun casts a golden glow over Geirangerfjord.
For a journey that feels personal, with every detail tailored to your preferences.

Family-Friendly: Adventures for All Ages
The Norwegian Fjords are an extraordinary destination for families, offering countless opportunities to create lasting memories. Cruises designed for families focus on accessibility, kid-friendly activities, and all-ages adventures that make the fjords an unforgettable playground.

Family-Friendly Features
1. Onboard Activities
Cruise lines like Norwegian Cruise Line (NCL), Royal Caribbean, and MSC Cruises cater to families with amenities like pools, water slides, climbing walls, and kids' clubs.
Example: NCL's ships feature Splash Academy, where children can join age-appropriate programs while parents enjoy quiet moments.

2. Spacious Accommodations
Family-friendly cabins range from interconnecting rooms to larger suites with multiple bedrooms and living spaces.
Price Range: €1,500–€2,500 per person for a 7-night itinerary in a family-friendly cabin.

3. Excursions for All Ages
Many fjord excursions are designed with families in mind, from gentle nature walks to wildlife safaris.
Examples:
- Fjord kayaking for beginners in Ålesund (€50–€70 per person).
- A ride on the Flåm Railway, one of the world's most scenic train journeys. Children often delight in the dramatic tunnels and waterfall stops (€60 per adult; discounted for children).

4. Cultural Experiences for Kids
Family cruises incorporate interactive activities like Viking reenactments in Gudvangen or hands-on cooking classes to learn how to make traditional Norwegian pancakes (pannekaker).
What I Observed: During a Viking-themed shore excursion, children dressed in tunics and wielded wooden swords while learning about Viking life. Watching their faces light up as they listened to stories of heroic voyages was heartwarming.

Why Choose Family-Friendly?
For the joy of watching your children marvel at puffins and seals, or seeing them gasp at the sight of towering waterfalls.
For the ease of balancing relaxation for adults with adventure for kids, ensuring everyone has the time of their life.

Budget Options: Experiencing the Fjords Without Breaking the Bank
The fjords' beauty isn't reserved for luxury travelers—there are countless ways to experience this magical destination on a budget. Budget cruising doesn't mean sacrificing the experience; it simply means embracing smart planning and making intentional choices to maximize value.

Budget-Friendly Features
1. Affordable Cruise Lines
Lines like MSC Cruises and Costa Cruises offer fjord itineraries at competitive prices, providing a comfortable and scenic experience without unnecessary frills.
Price Range: Starting at €1,000–€1,500 per person for a 7-night cruise.

2. Interior or Oceanview Cabins
Opting for an interior or oceanview cabin rather than a balcony suite can significantly lower costs.
Tip: Spend your time on deck or in public lounges to soak in the views. The fjords are just as breathtaking when shared with fellow passengers.

3. Self-Guided Shore Excursions
Skip organized excursions and explore ports independently. Many fjordside towns, such as Bergen and Ålesund, are walkable and offer free or low-cost attractions.
Examples:
- Hike to Mount Fløyen in Bergen (funicular ride: €15; hiking trail: free).
- Visit Ålesund's Art Nouveau Center (€10 entry).
- Pack a picnic and enjoy the beauty of fjordside parks.

4. Budget Dining
While onboard dining is included in most cruise fares, exploring local eateries during shore excursions can add variety without breaking the bank. Seek out fish markets and family-run cafés for affordable, authentic meals.
Example: Try fish cakes or traditional Norwegian waffles with jam at a local café for under €10.

What I Observed
Traveling on a budget fostered a sense of resourcefulness and connection. A simple picnic lunch by the banks of Geirangerfjord, paired with fresh bread, local cheese, and jam, became one of the most memorable meals of

my trip. It was a reminder that the fjords' magic doesn't come from luxury—it's inherent in their beauty.

Why Choose Budget Options?

- For the satisfaction of experiencing one of the world's most awe-inspiring destinations without financial stress.
- For the chance to get creative with your plans and uncover hidden gems along the way.

Chapter 3: Timing Your Adventure

Seasons in the Fjords

The Norwegian Fjords are nature's ultimate storyteller, with every season presenting a new chapter filled with unique sights, emotions, and experiences. These fjords, shaped over millennia by glaciers, are never stagnant—they morph, breathe, and evolve with the passage of time. From the glowing Midnight Sun to the ethereal Northern Lights, every season offers a distinct allure, transforming the fjords into a canvas painted anew by nature's hand.

Spring: A Rebirth of Life and Color (April to May)

Spring in the fjords is a season of awakening. As the snow begins to retreat from the cliffs and peaks, the landscapes burst into life with vibrant green meadows and colorful wildflowers. The air is crisp and refreshing, carrying the promise of summer's warmth.

What to Expect
- Blossoming Orchards: In regions like Hardangerfjord, the "Orchard of Norway," fruit trees awaken in an explosion of white and pink blossoms. This is an incredibly photogenic time, with rows of cherry, apple, and pear trees framing the still, emerald waters.
- Waterfalls in Full Flow: Melting snow feeds the waterfalls, making spring the best time to witness them at their

mightiest. Geirangerfjord's Seven Sisters waterfall roars with energy, cascading dramatically down the cliffs.
- Wildlife Spotting: Migratory birds return to the fjords, and seals and porpoises can often be seen basking near the shoreline.

Price and Crowds
Pricing: Cruises in spring are more affordable compared to summer, with itineraries starting around €1,000–€1,500 per person.
Crowds: Spring is a quieter season, perfect for those seeking a more tranquil experience.

My Experience
I still remember walking along a trail in Hardangerfjord, where the ground was carpeted with tiny flowers and the trees were heavy with blossoms. The scent of fruit blossoms mingled with the fresh, dewy air, and every step felt like breathing in the essence of spring. The waterfalls thundered in the distance, a constant reminder of the snowmelt feeding the fjord. It was as though nature herself was celebrating the rebirth of life.

Summer: The Midnight Sun and Vibrant Fjords (June to August)

Summer is the most popular time to visit the Norwegian Fjords, and it's easy to see why. The fjords come alive with long days and golden sunlight, making it a season of adventure, warmth, and boundless exploration.

What to Expect
- Midnight Sun: North of the Arctic Circle, the sun never sets during this season, bathing the landscape in a surreal, soft glow even in the middle of the night.
- Perfect Hiking Weather: Trails like Pulpit Rock (Preikestolen) above Lysefjord are accessible and ideal for outdoor enthusiasts. The meadows are lush, the skies clear, and the fjords calm—a hiker's paradise.
- Boat Cruises and Kayaking: The calm, mirror-like fjord waters make summer perfect for kayaking. Nærøyfjord, in particular, feels like a dream as you paddle through its serene, narrow passages.
- Vibrant Festivals: Towns and villages along the fjords celebrate local traditions, from Viking reenactments to outdoor markets filled with Norwegian delicacies.

Price and Crowds
Pricing: Summer is peak season, with cruises ranging from €2,000 to €4,000 per person depending on the itinerary and cabin type.
Crowds: Popular ports like Bergen and Geirangerfjord can be bustling, but the energy is infectious.

My Experience
Sailing through Geirangerfjord in July, I stood on the ship's deck at midnight, bathed in sunlight as golden as dawn's first light. The cliffs rose around me, their edges softened by wildflowers clinging to the crevices. Later, hiking to Pulpit Rock, I marveled at the sheer drop into Lysefjord below. The air was warm, the sky impossibly blue, and every step felt alive with possibility. It was as though the fjords themselves had opened their arms, inviting us to bask in their glory.

Autumn: A Tapestry of Colors (September to October)

Autumn in the fjords is a season of transformation. The landscapes, once vibrant green, take on hues of fiery red, burnt orange, and golden yellow. This season brings a sense of intimacy and reflection, as the bustle of summer gives way to quieter days.

What to Expect
- Fall Foliage: The forests and fjordside villages are painted in autumn colors, creating a breathtaking contrast against the deep blue waters.
- Fresh Harvests: Markets come alive with freshly picked apples, pears, and berries from the local orchards, alongside artisanal cheeses and honey.
- Hiking Under Golden Light: Trails like those around Romsdalseggen Ridge offer panoramic views of fjords framed by autumn leaves.
- Cool, Clear Skies: September often brings the year's clearest skies, perfect for stargazing and soaking in the natural beauty.

Price and Crowds
- Pricing: Autumn cruises are more affordable than summer, typically starting at €1,200–€1,800 per person.
- Crowds: Fewer tourists visit during this season, offering a more peaceful experience.

My Experience
On an October morning in Flåm, I hiked up a path lined with trees whose leaves glowed like embers in the sunlight. As I reached the viewpoint, the fjord stretched out below, perfectly calm and reflecting the kaleidoscope of colors above it. Later that day, I wandered through an orchard, plucking ripe apples that were bursting with sweetness. The world felt quieter, more introspective, and I found myself deeply connected to the rhythm of the season.

Winter: A Frozen Wonderland and the Northern Lights (November to March)

Winter transforms the fjords into an Arctic wonderland. With snow-covered peaks, frozen waterfalls, and the mesmerizing Northern Lights, this is the season of magic and enchantment.

What to Expect
- Snow-Covered Landscapes: The fjords take on an ethereal beauty, with snowy cliffs reflecting the pale winter light.
- Northern Lights: From ports like Tromsø or Alta, winter cruises often include opportunities to witness the aurora borealis dancing across the Arctic sky.
- Winter Sports: Dog sledding, snowshoeing, and even cross-country skiing are popular winter activities.
- Cozy Atmosphere: Villages along the fjords twinkle with fairy lights, and cafés serve warm drinks like Norwegian hot chocolate and mulled wine.

Price and Crowds
- Pricing: Winter is the most budget-friendly season, with cruises starting at €800–€1,500 per person.

- Crowds: The fjords are serene and less visited, making winter an intimate and magical time.

My Experience
In the heart of Tromsø's fjord, I stood bundled in layers, staring up at the night sky as it came alive with ribbons of green, pink, and purple. The Northern Lights felt like a dance—a performance just for us. During the day, I explored frozen fjordside trails, the crunch of snow beneath my boots breaking the silence. Each village welcomed us with warm smiles and crackling fires, making the icy cold outside feel like an invitation to savor life's simplest joys.

Month-by-month breakdown of what to expect

The Norwegian Fjords are a masterpiece in flux, constantly transformed by the rhythm of the seasons. No two months are the same here, as light, weather, and landscapes weave a changing tapestry that invites you to experience a different kind of magic depending on when you visit. Whether you're chasing the Northern Lights, hiking under the Midnight Sun, or marveling at roaring spring waterfalls, every month offers its own distinct beauty.

January: A Snow-Covered Wonderland
What to Expect:
The fjords are blanketed in snow, and the air is crisp and serene. Waterfalls may be frozen into icy sculptures, and the surrounding cliffs shimmer under the pale winter sun. This is peak time for the Northern Lights, particularly in regions like Tromsø or Alta.
Activities:
- Northern Lights safaris: Join guided tours to chase the aurora (€100–€150).
- Dog sledding or snowshoeing: Glide across frozen fjords or explore snow-covered trails (€70–€120).
- Winter photography workshops: Capture the icy beauty of the fjords.

What I Observed:
On a January night in Tromsø, the sky suddenly came alive with ribbons of green and purple light—like the heavens themselves were dancing. I watched in awe, feeling a mix of wonder and deep gratitude to witness such a moment.
Pricing:
January is low season for cruises, with fares starting around €800–€1,200 per person.

February: Arctic Serenity and Sami Culture
What to Expect:
The quiet of winter continues, but February brings slightly longer days and vivid sunsets. This is an excellent time to learn about Sami culture and traditions in northern regions.
Activities:

- Reindeer sledding: Ride through snow-covered landscapes guided by Sami herders (€100–€200).
- Sami cultural experiences: Enjoy storytelling, traditional food, and joik (Sami singing).

What I Observed:
Sitting in a Sami lavvu (tent) under a blanket of stars, I listened to an elder recount the legends of her ancestors. The warmth of the fire, combined with the icy air outside, created a moment of profound connection.

Pricing:
Similar to January, with opportunities for discounted cruise fares in the €800–€1,500 range.

March: Emerging Light and Winter's Last Dance

What to Expect:
Winter begins to loosen its grip, and daylight hours noticeably increase. The snow-covered peaks glisten under the brighter sun, and wildlife becomes more active.

Activities:
- Cross-country skiing: Glide through scenic fjordside trails (€60–€100).
- Northern Lights tours: March is one of the last months to see the aurora.

What to Observe:
The interplay of light and shadow on the cliffs—longer days illuminate the peaks in golden hues while the fjords remain in deep blue shade.

Pricing:
Still within low-season ranges, making it a great time for budget-conscious travelers.

April: The Awakening of Spring

What to Expect:
April is a month of transition. While snow still lingers on the mountaintops, the lower valleys begin to thaw, and waterfalls roar to life from the snowmelt. Spring flowers start to bloom in Hardangerfjord.

Activities:
- Scenic cruises through awakening fjords (€1,000–€1,500 per person).
- Hiking lower-altitude trails: Discover wildflowers and newly vibrant landscapes.

What I Observed:
Cruising through Nærøyfjord in April, I saw waterfalls cascading with newfound vigor, their mist catching the sunlight and creating tiny rainbows. It felt as though the fjords themselves were celebrating the arrival of spring.

Pricing:
Shoulder-season rates offer excellent value, with fewer crowds and affordable shore excursions.

May: Blossoms and Waterfalls

What to Expect:
May is one of the most breathtaking months in the fjords. Hardangerfjord transforms into a floral wonderland as orchards bloom, and the waterfalls are at their peak.

Activities:
- Explore Hardangerfjord's blossoming orchards (€30–€50 for guided tours).
- Visit cultural sites: May is Norway's Constitution Month, with celebrations and parades in fjordside towns.

What I Observed:
Walking through rows of blooming cherry trees along Hardangerfjord, I was intoxicated by the floral scent mingling with the cool breeze from the water. The snowcapped peaks

in the background made the scene feel like a dream.
Pricing:
Prices begin to rise as the summer season approaches, with cruises starting at €1,200–€1,800.

June: The Midnight Sun's Arrival
What to Expect:
June marks the start of the summer season, with long daylight hours and mild weather. The Midnight Sun illuminates the northern fjords, allowing you to hike, kayak, and explore around the clock.
Activities:
Kayaking in Nærøyfjord or Geirangerfjord (€70–€100 per person).
Midnight Sun safaris north of the Arctic Circle.
What I Observed:
At midnight in Tromsø, I stood on a cliff watching the sun dip toward the horizon but never fully set. It bathed the fjord in golden light, and I marveled at the surreal beauty of a night that never truly became dark.
Pricing:
Peak-season rates kick in, with cruises ranging from €2,000–€4,000 per person.

July: Summer in Full Bloom
What to Expect:
July is the height of summer, with lush greenery, buzzing villages, and calm fjord waters. Outdoor adventures are at their peak, making it the best time for active travelers.
Activities:
Hike to Preikestolen (Pulpit Rock) above Lysefjord.
Join local festivals celebrating Norwegian culture.

Pricing:
Peak season continues, with high demand for balcony cabins.

August: Lush Landscapes and Golden Light
What to Expect:
Summer begins to wane, and the light takes on a softer, golden quality. The fjords remain warm and lively but less crowded than July.
Activities:
- Boat cruises showcasing the fjords' grandeur (€70–€120).
- Wildlife watching: Spot puffins, seals, and whales.

Pricing:
Still within the peak-season price range.

September: The First Signs of Autumn
What to Expect:
Leaves begin to change color, and the fjords take on a warm, golden glow. September often brings the clearest skies of the year.
Activities:
- Stargazing: With darker nights returning, stargazing becomes a magical experience.
- Fjordside picnics: Enjoy freshly harvested apples and cheeses.

Pricing:
Prices start to drop, with cruises averaging €1,200–€2,000.

October: Autumn's Kaleidoscope
What to Expect:
The fall colors are at their peak, and the fjords are serene and quiet. October is a month of reflection, perfect for those seeking tranquility.
Activities:
Explore fjordside trails under autumn leaves.

Visit small villages for cozy, authentic experiences.
What to Observe:
The vivid reflections of autumn foliage on the still water create postcard-perfect scenes.
Pricing:
Shoulder-season prices make this an excellent time for budget travelers.

November: The Quiet Before Winter
What to Expect:
The days grow shorter, and the fjords become quiet and introspective. Frost begins to dust the cliffs, and the first hints of winter appear.
Activities:
- Short hikes in frosty conditions.
- Local storytelling evenings in small villages.

Pricing:
Winter pricing begins, offering budget-friendly options.

December: Festive Fjords
What to Expect:
The fjords sparkle with festive lights as villages celebrate Christmas. Snow blankets the region, and the Northern Lights begin their winter performance.
Activities:
- Christmas markets in Bergen and Ålesund.
- Northern Lights cruises (€800–€1,500).

What I Observed:
Walking through Bergen's Christmas market, sipping gløgg (mulled wine), I felt the warmth of the holiday spirit even in the frosty air. It was a magical way to welcome winter in the fjords.

Weather, wildlife, and cultural highlights

Few places in the world hold the magic of the Norwegian Fjords—a realm where shifting weather transforms the landscape into living art, where wildlife thrives in harmony with its surroundings, and where culture dances through centuries of history. Every element here feels interconnected: the soft mist on the water, the call of a distant eagle, and the melody of Norwegian folk songs. To truly immerse yourself in this extraordinary destination, you must experience its weather, marvel at its wildlife, and embrace its cultural soul.

The Weather: The Ever-Changing Artist
The weather in the Norwegian Fjords is like a painter at work—constantly blending hues, shifting light, and creating masterpieces that are as fleeting as they are stunning. Its

unpredictability is part of its charm, and every moment feels like stepping into a new scene.

What to Expect
Spring (April-May):
Spring heralds the return of life as snow melts from the peaks and lush greenery carpets the valleys. Temperatures range from 5°C to 15°C (41°F to 59°F), and waterfalls cascade with renewed vigor. Expect a mix of sunny days, refreshing rain showers, and occasional mist that adds an ethereal quality to the fjords.

My Observation: During an April hike along Hardangerfjord, the skies alternated between bursts of sunshine and light drizzle. The scent of fresh rain mingled with blooming wildflowers, and every raindrop on the leaves seemed to glisten like a tiny jewel.

Summer (June-August):
With long daylight hours and temperatures from 10°C to 25°C (50°F to 77°F), summer is the most stable and vibrant season. Clear skies dominate, but sporadic rains can add dramatic clouds to your photos.

What to Look For: Watch for soft, golden light during the Midnight Sun, especially in northern fjords like Tromsø. It paints the cliffs and water in shades of amber and rose.

Autumn (September-October):
Autumn's palette is rich and warm, with leaves turning fiery shades of red, orange, and yellow. Crisp, cool air (5°C to 15°C or 41°F to 59°F) and misty mornings create a sense of tranquility.

My Observation: On an October morning in Geirangerfjord, I watched mist rise from the water, slowly revealing the vibrant foliage reflected like a mirror. It felt like watching the world wake up, one color at a time.

Winter (November-March):
Winter transforms the fjords into a wonderland of snow-covered cliffs, frozen waterfalls, and icy waters. Temperatures range from -5°C to 5°C (23°F to 41°F), and the Northern Lights bring a celestial spectacle to the night skies.

What to Feel: The chill of winter is balanced by the warmth of cozy fires in fjordside cottages, where you can sip hot chocolate as snowflakes drift past the windows.

The Wildlife: A Thriving Ecosystem
The fjords are alive with wildlife, from the sky above to the waters below, offering a chance to connect with nature in its purest form. Observing these creatures in their natural habitat is a reminder of the interconnectedness of all life.

What to Observe
Marine Life:
- Whales: Orcas, humpback whales, and minke whales are frequent visitors to fjord waters, particularly during winter migrations. Whale-watching tours from Tromsø or Andenes (€100–€150) often bring you face-to-face with these majestic beings.
- Seals and Porpoises: These playful creatures can often be spotted lounging on rocks or gliding through the water near the shoreline.

Birdlife:
- White-Tailed Eagles: Known as "sea eagles," these impressive birds glide effortlessly above the fjords, their

piercing calls echoing through the cliffs.
- Puffins: Nesting on coastal cliffs in spring and summer, these adorable seabirds with their bright orange beaks are a delight to watch. Bird-watching tours (€50–€70) in regions like Runde Island or Vesterålen are highly recommended.

Land Animals:
Reindeer: Particularly in northern fjords, reindeer can be seen grazing in tundra landscapes. Reindeer sledding excursions (€100–€200) offer a unique way to observe them up close.
Arctic Foxes and Moose: Rare but thrilling sightings in more remote areas.

My Experience
One summer morning, kayaking through Nærøyfjord, I spotted a pod of porpoises playfully swimming alongside my group. The fjord was so calm that their every movement sent ripples across the surface, breaking the stillness in the most enchanting way. Later, as we rounded a bend, a white-tailed eagle soared overhead, its powerful wings cutting through the air. It was a moment of pure connection with the wild.

The Cultural Highlights: A Tapestry of Heritage
The culture of the Norwegian Fjords is as rich as the landscapes themselves—a blend of Viking legacy, coastal traditions, and a deep connection to nature. Exploring this culture is as much a part of the journey as the fjords themselves.

Festivals and Traditions
Syttende Mai (May 17th): Norway's Constitution Day is celebrated with parades, traditional music, and folk costumes (bunads). Towns like Bergen and Ålesund come alive with festivities.
What to Experience: Join the locals in singing the national anthem and waving Norwegian flags as the parades wind through charming streets.

Viking Heritage:
Visit Viking museums in towns like Gudvangen, where you can explore reconstructed longhouses and experience Viking life through storytelling and reenactments (€20–€30).
My Experience: Sitting by a roaring fire in Gudvangen, I listened to a storyteller recount the adventures of Norse gods. The crackling flames seemed to echo the fierce spirit of the Vikings, making the legends feel alive.

Sami Culture:
Northern fjords offer opportunities to connect with Sami traditions, including joik singing, reindeer herding, and tasting traditional dishes like bidos (reindeer stew).

Music and Arts
- Fjordside Folk Music: The haunting tunes of the Hardingfele (Hardanger fiddle) reflect the fjords' natural beauty. Attend a live performance in small villages for an authentic experience.
- Art Galleries: The dramatic landscapes have inspired countless artists, and galleries in Bergen and Flåm showcase stunning works.

Final Thoughts

the Norwegian Fjords are more than just a destination—they are a living, breathing masterpiece shaped by weather, inhabited by wildlife, and enriched by culture. Every moment spent here feels like a conversation with nature and history, a dialogue that leaves you in awe of the world's beauty and diversity.

As you explore the fjords, take time to feel the weather, listen for the call of an eagle, and dance to the rhythm of Norwegian folk music. The stories of the fjords are woven into every gust of wind, every ripple in the water, and every smile from the people who call this extraordinary place home.

Chapter 4: Packing Essentials

The ultimate packing list for all seasons

Packing for a journey to the Norwegian Fjords is like preparing for an epic adventure—it's exciting, yes, but also a balancing act between practicality and comfort. With a climate as dynamic as the landscapes themselves, and adventures ranging from leisurely strolls to kayaking beneath waterfalls, the right packing strategy can make all the difference. Each season in the fjords presents its own distinct personality, meaning your packing list must adapt accordingly.

General Packing Essentials (For All Seasons)
Before we dive into seasonal specifics, there are a few items that are indispensable regardless of when you visit:
1. Layers, Layers, Layers

The weather in the fjords is famously unpredictable—you could feel warm sunshine one moment and encounter a brisk wind or drizzle the next. Layering is key:
- Base Layer: Thermal or moisture-wicking tops and leggings (starting at €20–€50). These keep you warm in winter and comfortable in summer.
- Mid-Layer: A fleece or lightweight sweater (€40–€80).
- Outer Layer: A waterproof and windproof jacket (€100–€200). Look for breathable yet durable options for hiking or outdoor activities.

2. Comfortable Footwear
- Hiking Boots: Invest in sturdy, waterproof hiking boots with good

ankle support (€80–€150). Even easy trails can be rocky or muddy.
- Casual Shoes: Lightweight, comfortable sneakers or walking shoes for exploring towns (€50–€100).

My Observation: I'll never forget climbing to Pulpit Rock in boots that hugged my ankles like a second skin. The comfort transformed what could have been a grueling hike into an effortless adventure.

3. Backpack
A daypack (20–30 liters, €50–€100) is essential for carrying snacks, water, a camera, and extra layers during excursions. Look for one with a rain cover.

4. Reusable Water Bottle
The water in Norway is pristine and drinkable, so a refillable bottle (€15–€30) is a must. Staying hydrated is crucial for hikes.

5. Essentials for Rainy Days
- Compact Travel Umbrella: Lightweight and wind-resistant (€10–€30).
- Waterproof Backpack Cover or Dry Bags: Protects your belongings from unexpected rain (€15–€25).

6. Electronics
- Universal Travel Adapter: Norway uses type C or F plugs (€10–€20).
- Power Bank: Essential for long excursions (€20–€50).
- Camera Gear: A good camera or smartphone with plenty of storage to capture the fjords' beauty.

7. Personal Health and Safety
- Sunscreen: Yes, even in winter! The reflection off the water or snow can intensify UV rays (€10–€20).
- Bug Spray: For summer visits, especially near forests or lakes (€5–€10).
- First Aid Kit: Include blister plasters for long hikes (€10–€25).

Packing for Spring (April-May)
Spring in the fjords is a time of rebirth—snow melts, waterfalls roar, and valleys transform into lush green havens. The weather, however, can be unpredictable, swinging between sunshine, rain, and occasional frost.

Key Items for Spring
1. **Waterproof Boots:** Trails can be muddy due to snowmelt.
2. **Light Gloves and Hat**: For those brisk mornings and windy hikes.
3. **Rain Pants:** To keep you dry during sudden showers (€30–€70).
4. **Binoculars**: A must for birdwatchers, as migratory birds return to nest (€50–€150).

<u>**Clothing Observations**</u>
In April, I packed a lightweight thermal base layer under my hiking outfit and was glad I did—early mornings in Hardangerfjord felt almost icy, yet the afternoons warmed enough for me to shed layers comfortably.

<u>**Packing for Summer (June-August)**</u>

Summer is the most stable season in the fjords, with long daylight hours and comfortable temperatures. However, it's still wise to pack for occasional rain and cooler evenings.

Key Items for Summer
1. **Breathable Activewear**: For hiking or kayaking. Quick-dry tops and pants are ideal (€20–€60).
2. **Sunhat and Sunglasses**: For shielding against the glare of the Midnight Sun (€15–€50).
3. **Swimwear**: Many fjord cruises or accommodations have hot tubs, and some brave souls even swim in the fjords!
4. **Lightweight** Sleeping Mask: If you're north of the Arctic Circle, the Midnight Sun means the skies never darken completely (€10–€15).

Clothing Observations
One balmy July day in Geirangerfjord, I wore a short-sleeved shirt and hiking shorts while kayaking beneath cascading waterfalls. Later that evening, on the ship deck, a fleece was all I needed to keep warm as the sun lingered low on the horizon.

Packing for Autumn (September-October)
Autumn in the fjords is a symphony of colors—red, orange, and gold leaves reflected in the water. The air grows crisp, and cooler temperatures call for warmer layers.

Key Items for Autumn
1. **Warm Scarf and Beanie Hat:** Add an extra layer of coziness (€20–€40).
2. **Insulated Vest or Jacket:** Mornings and evenings can be chilly (€50–€150).
3. **Sturdy Hiking Socks:** Wool blends are perfect for keeping your feet warm and blister-free (€10–€20).
4. **Thermal Flask:** For carrying hot drinks on hikes (€15–€30).

Clothing Observations
As I walked through an autumnal forest in Flåm, the crunch of leaves underfoot added to the sensory delight. Layers allowed me to enjoy the brisk air without feeling too cold as I paused to savor the vibrant colors.

Packing for Winter (November-March)
Winter transforms the fjords into an icy paradise, perfect for Northern Lights chasers and lovers of snowy landscapes. Packing for extreme cold is key.

Key Items for Winter
1. **Thermal Base Layers**: Essential for insulation against freezing temperatures (€20–€50).
2. **Heavy-Duty Waterproof Jacket**: Look for down or synthetic insulation (€150–€300).
3. **Waterproof Snow Boots**: Insulated, non-slip boots are a lifesaver for icy trails (€100–€200).
4. **Gloves, Scarf, and Thermal Hat**: Opt for windproof materials (€50–€100 for the set).
5. **Hand Warmers:** Perfect for pockets or gloves (€5–€10 for a pack).

Clothing Observations
On a winter night in Tromsø, dressed in my heaviest parka and boots, I gazed at the Northern Lights. Though the cold was intense, layers and hand warmers kept me warm enough to savor the celestial display without distraction.

Extras for a Perfect Fjord Cruise
- Journal or Sketchbook**:** Capture your reflections and sketches inspired by the stunning landscapes (€10–€30).

- Local Guidebook: Having a guide to flora, fauna, or cultural history enriches the experience (€15–€25).
- Norwegian Phrases App or Booklet: Learn key phrases like "Takk" (thank you) to connect with locals.

Dressing for unpredictable weather in the Fjords

Exploring the Norwegian Fjords is like stepping into an epic storybook—one filled with jagged peaks, shimmering waters, and endless adventure. From hiking beneath cascading waterfalls to capturing the perfect photo of a white-tailed eagle soaring above the cliffs, every moment in the fjords feels alive with possibility. But to fully embrace this extraordinary experience, you'll need the right accessories by your side. These seemingly small items can make a world of difference, transforming a good day into an unforgettable one.

Accessories for Hiking: Navigating the Trails with Confidence

Hiking in the Norwegian Fjords is more than just a physical activity—it's a chance to immerse yourself in the raw beauty of nature. Whether you're scaling the heights of Pulpit Rock or strolling along a gentle fjord-side path, the right accessories will ensure you stay comfortable, prepared, and connected to the landscapes around you.

1. Trekking Poles

Why You Need Them: The trails in the fjords can range from smooth to rugged, often with steep inclines, loose rocks, or muddy patches. Trekking poles provide stability, reduce strain on your knees, and make uphill climbs less exhausting.

What to Look For: Lightweight, collapsible poles with adjustable lengths (€30–€80).

Personal Anecdote: On a hike along the Romsdalseggen Ridge, I saw a fellow hiker slip on a gravelly slope, only to catch themselves with their trekking poles. That moment reinforced how invaluable they can be, especially on uneven terrain.

2. Hydration Bladder or Bottle

Why You Need It: Staying hydrated is non-negotiable, especially during long hikes. A hydration bladder fits conveniently into your backpack, allowing you to sip water through a tube without stopping.

Price Range: €20–€60, depending on size (1–3 liters).

Observation: During a hike to Trolltunga, I noticed that those with hydration bladders moved more seamlessly up the trail compared to those who constantly paused to grab water bottles from their bags. It's a small convenience that makes a big difference.

3. Headlamp

Why You Need It: In the fjords, twilight can linger late into the night during summer, but conditions can still turn dim on foggy or overcast days. A headlamp is essential for early starts or if you find yourself descending a trail as dusk falls.

What to Look For: Lightweight models with adjustable brightness settings (€20–€50).

Personal Experience: On a spring evening hike near Geirangerfjord, I underestimated how quickly the fog could roll in. Thankfully, my headlamp illuminated the trail, guiding me safely back down while adding an adventurous glow to the surroundings.

4. Waterproof Dry Bags
Why You Need Them: Sudden rain showers are common in the fjords. Dry bags ensure your essentials (phone, camera, snacks) stay safe and dry.
Price Range: €15–€40, depending on size (5–30 liters).
What I Observed: Crossing a misty stream on the hike to Kjeragbolten, I was grateful my camera was tucked securely in a dry bag. A friend's unprotected gear wasn't as lucky—lesson learned.

Accessories for Photography: Capturing the Fjords' Timeless Beauty

In the Norwegian Fjords, every angle tells a story, and every scene begs to be captured. With the right photography accessories, you can preserve these moments with clarity and creativity.

1. Tripod
Why You Need It: A sturdy tripod is essential for capturing long-exposure shots of waterfalls, the Northern Lights, or the fjords during twilight.
What to Look For: Lightweight, travel-friendly tripods with flexible legs (€50–€150).
Personal Anecdote: At the base of the Seven Sisters waterfall in Geirangerfjord, I set up my tripod to capture the cascading water in soft, silky detail. The photo became one of my favorites—not just for the result, but for the memory of steadying my hands in the midst of the fjord's roaring beauty.

2. Polarizing Lens Filter
Why You Need It: A polarizing filter reduces glare from water and enhances the contrast in skies, making your photos of the fjords even more dramatic.
Price Range: €20–€80, depending on lens size.
Observation: As I photographed the still waters of Sognefjord, the polarizing filter brought out reflections of the cliffs with stunning clarity. It made the difference between a good shot and one that took my breath away.

3. Extra Batteries and Memory Cards
Why You Need Them: Cold temperatures and long shooting days can drain batteries faster than usual. Bring extras to avoid missing key moments.
Price Range:
Batteries: €20–€50 each.
Memory Cards: €10–€30 for high-capacity options.
What I Experienced: During a winter Northern Lights tour near Tromsø, my camera's battery died just as the lights intensified. Thankfully, I had a spare, allowing me to capture the aurora's swirling ribbons of green and purple.

4. Camera Rain Cover
Why You Need It: Sudden rain or mist from waterfalls can damage your gear. A lightweight rain cover protects your camera while allowing you to keep shooting.
Price Range: €15–€30.
Personal Reflection: Standing on deck during a rainy fjord cruise, I watched raindrops bead on my camera's rain cover while still capturing moody, atmospheric shots. It was a small

investment that paid off in unforgettable images.

Accessories for Cruise Life: Relaxation and Exploration

Cruise life in the fjords is about finding a balance between indulgence and adventure. These accessories will help you make the most of your time on board and during shore excursions.

1. Binoculars
Why You Need Them: Whether you're spotting white-tailed eagles soaring above the cliffs or seals lounging on rocky outcrops, binoculars bring the fjord's wildlife closer.
What to Look For: Compact models with waterproofing and 8x–10x magnification (€50–€150).
Personal Anecdote: On a lazy afternoon aboard a ship in Nærøyfjord, I used my binoculars to trace an eagle's flight as it glided between crags. Sharing the moment with fellow passengers created an impromptu bond of shared wonder.

2. Deck Blanket or Travel Wrap
Why You Need It: Even summer evenings can feel cool out on the deck. A cozy blanket or wrap lets you linger longer beneath the stars or the Midnight Sun.
Price Range: €20–€60, depending on material (wool or fleece).

3. Reusable Coffee Mug
Why You Need It: Sipping hot coffee or tea as you watch waterfalls slip past is one of cruise life's simple pleasures. A reusable mug also reduces waste.
Price Range: €15–€30.

What I Observed: On a brisk morning cruise through Lysefjord, the warmth of my coffee, cradled in a sturdy travel mug, felt like a hug in liquid form. It paired perfectly with the sight of mist lifting off the water.

4. Comfortable Binocular Straps
Long days on excursions mean that heavy binoculars can become cumbersome. Invest in padded straps (€10–€30) for ultimate comfort during wildlife tours.

5. Journal or Sketchbook
Why You Need It: The fjords inspire reflection, and a journal lets you capture your thoughts, sketches, or even pressed flowers from the trails.
Price Range: €10–€25.
What I Experienced: One twilight evening, sitting on the deck of a cruise ship in Bergen, I sketched the outline of the harbor's colorful houses. Though my drawing was simple, it became a lasting reminder of the peace I felt in that moment.

Must-have accessories for hiking, photography, and cruise life

Must-Have Accessories for Hiking, Photography, and Cruise Life in the Norwegian The Norwegian Fjords have a way of igniting your senses like few places on Earth. The towering cliffs, cascading waterfalls, and mirror-like waters seem to invite both exploration and reverence. But to fully immerse yourself in the majesty of this extraordinary region, you'll want to travel prepared—not just with the right clothing, but also with the accessories that enhance every aspect of your journey. These aren't just things to pack; they're tools to help you savor each moment, no matter where the trail, camera lens, or cruise deck takes you.

1. Accessories for Hiking: Embrace Adventure Fully Prepared

Whether you're embarking on a strenuous hike to Pulpit Rock or wandering along the tranquil paths of a fjord-side village, the right accessories will make every step as comfortable and memorable as possible.

a. Trekking Poles

Why They're Essential: The trails in the fjords can be steep, uneven, and occasionally slippery. Trekking poles are invaluable for providing stability, especially on descents, and reducing the impact on your knees.
Features to Look For: Adjustable, lightweight aluminum or carbon fiber poles, preferably collapsible (€30–€80).
Personal Moment: On the ascent to Romsdalseggen Ridge, I was grateful for my trekking poles. The inclines felt less intimidating, and I could focus on the view instead of the effort. They became, quite literally, my supportive companions.

b. Waterproof Boots

Why They're Essential: The trails often lead through patches of wet grass, muddy stretches, and rocky terrain. Waterproof boots protect your feet from dampness and keep your footing steady.
Features to Look For: High ankle support, durable soles with good grip, and breathable lining (€80–€150).
Observation: On a rainy spring hike in Hardangerfjord, my boots kept my feet dry even as the trail turned into a small stream. A fellow traveler in non-waterproof shoes ended up with soaked feet—a stark reminder of this necessity.

c. Daypack with Hydration System

Why It's Essential: A comfortable, lightweight backpack lets you carry essentials like snacks, water, extra layers, and a first-aid kit.
Features to Look For: Look for a 20–30L capacity, with a hydration bladder for easy sipping on the move (€50–€100).
Tip: A rain cover or waterproof daypack will save your gear during unexpected showers.

d. Headlamp

Why It's Essential: If your hike takes longer than expected or if you begin during the soft light of dawn, a headlamp ensures safety on dim or foggy trails.
Recommended Features: Brightness settings and adjustable straps (€20–€50).
Personal Story: Descending from Kjeragbolten under a misty sky, my headlamp pierced the gathering gloom, lighting my way while adding a touch of adventure to the quiet descent.

e. Gaiters

Why They're Essential: Gaiters keep water, mud, and small rocks out of your boots, especially on messy or challenging trails.
Price Range: €15–€50.

f. Snacks and Containers

Why They're Essential: High-energy snacks like nuts, trail mix, or protein bars can be lifesavers on longer hikes.

Observation: I carried a collapsible food container on a hike in Geirangerfjord, which allowed me to enjoy a leisurely lunch by the water. Storing leftovers in it was both practical and eco-friendly.

2. Accessories for Photography: Capturing the Majesty of the Fjords

Everywhere you look in the fjords, there's a scene begging to be captured. To make the most of this photographic paradise, the right accessories are as crucial as the camera itself.

a. Sturdy Tripod

Why It's Essential: For long-exposure shots of waterfalls or the Northern Lights, a tripod is a must to eliminate camera shake.
Features to Look For: Lightweight yet stable models, preferably travel-sized and foldable (€50–€150).
Personal Story: On a chilly morning in Sognefjord, I set my tripod along the fjord's edge to capture the cliffs' reflection. The stillness of the water, combined with the soft pastel hues of sunrise, made for an image that felt almost otherworldly.

b. Polarizing Lens Filter

Why It's Essential: Reduces glare from water and enhances the vividness of the landscape, making skies richer and reflections clearer.
Price Range: €20–€80.
What I Observed: Adding a polarizing filter allowed me to cut through the glare on Lysefjord, revealing the underwater details near the shoreline. The effect was mesmerizing.

c. Protective Camera Rain Cover

Why It's Essential: Sudden rain showers are common in the fjords, and a rain cover keeps your gear safe while you keep shooting.
Price Range: €10–€25.
Personal Reflection: Shooting photos near the Seven Sisters waterfall during a light drizzle, I watched the droplets bead off my camera's cover, grateful I could focus on composition rather than shielding my lens.

d. Backup Batteries and Storage Cards

Why They're Essential: Cold weather drains batteries quickly, and fjord landscapes inspire continuous shooting—so spares are a must.
Tip: Keep extra batteries in an inner pocket to keep them warm and extend their life.

e. Lightweight Camera Bag

Why It's Essential: A protective yet portable camera bag ensures you can carry your equipment comfortably during excursions.

3. Accessories for Cruise Life: Comfort and Enjoyment Afloat

Cruising the fjords is a unique blend of relaxation and exploration. These accessories will help you make the most of life on the water.

a. Binoculars

Why They're Essential: The Norwegian Fjords are a haven for wildlife. From spotting sea eagles above the cliffs to watching seals bask on rocky outcrops, binoculars bring you closer to the action.
Features to Look For: Waterproof models with 8x–10x magnification (€50–€150).
Personal Moment: Scanning the cliffs of Trollfjord, I spotted an eagle perched high

above. Sharing the sight with fellow passengers through my binoculars became a highlight of the day.

b. Travel Blanket
Why It's Essential: On cool evenings, as the sun dips behind the fjord's peaks, a soft blanket ensures you can linger on deck in comfort.
Price Range: €20–€50.

c. Reusable Water Bottle or Thermos
Why It's Essential: A water bottle keeps you hydrated during excursions, while a thermos is perfect for sipping hot coffee or tea as you watch the world drift by.
Personal Reflection: Sitting on the ship's bow one crisp morning, cradling a mug of steaming cocoa, I watched waterfalls tumble into the fjord. It was one of those rare moments of peace that stayed with me long after the journey ended.

d. Deck-Friendly Slip-Resistant Shoes
Why They're Essential: Non-slip soles are vital for safety on wet cruise decks.
Options and Price Range: Waterproof slip-on shoes (€30–€80).

e. Noise-Canceling Headphones
Why They're Essential: Perfect for those quiet moments when you want to enjoy soft music or listen to an audiobook as the fjords unfold around you.

Final Thoughts
accessories may seem small, but they carry the power to enhance every facet of your Norwegian Fjords adventure. The right trekking poles can make a steep climb feel effortless. A polarizing lens can turn an ordinary photo into a masterpiece. Binoculars can transform distant cliffs into intimate wildlife encounters. Every item you pack is not just practical—it's part of crafting moments you'll treasure forever.

Chapter 5: Iconic Fjords and Stunning Landscapes

Geirangerfjord: The breathtaking jewel

There are places in the world that feel as though they have been plucked straight from the realm of myth and magic. Geirangerfjord, with its towering cliffs, emerald waters, and cascading waterfalls, is one such place. Nestled in the heart of Norway, it stands not only as a UNESCO World Heritage Site but as a living testament to the raw, awe-inspiring power of nature. It is, without exaggeration, one of the most breathtaking places I have ever experienced—a jewel in the crown of the Norwegian Fjords.

Allow me to take you through every aspect of this magical destination, from its iconic landmarks to the subtle moments that make it unforgettable. I'll share the sights, the emotions, and those small details you might otherwise miss, weaving in personal anecdotes that bring Geirangerfjord to life.

The First Glimpse: A Landscape That Leaves You Speechless

As your cruise ship glides into Geirangerfjord, the cliffs begin to rise dramatically on either side, as if the Earth itself is wrapping you in an embrace. The air feels different here—crisper, tinged with the scent of pine and mist. The fjord's waters are so still, they mirror the cliffs above, creating the illusion of a world turned upside down. Every ripple sends a whisper across the water, breaking the silence in the gentlest of ways.

What to Observe

- The Seven Sisters Waterfall: These seven cascades tumble gracefully down the cliffs in parallel streams, resembling silver ribbons. Opposite them stands the Suitor, a solitary waterfall that, according to legend, courts the Seven Sisters.
- The Cliffs: Sheer and rugged, the cliffs are carpeted with a mosaic of green trees and patches of wildflowers, with farmhouses clinging improbably to their slopes.

What I Felt: My heart skipped a beat the moment I caught sight of the Seven Sisters. The symmetry of their fall seemed too perfect for nature alone, as though they had been designed to inspire awe.

Exploring Geirangerfjord: A Wonderland of Activities

From serene cruises to thrilling hikes, Geirangerfjord offers experiences for every kind of traveler. Whether you're seeking adventure or tranquility, there is magic to be found at every turn.

Fjord Cruises

Why It's a Must: Sailing the fjord's waters allows you to fully appreciate its grandeur. You can cruise past waterfalls, spot wildlife, and marvel at the reflection of the cliffs on the water.

Options:
- Short sightseeing cruises (1–2 hours, €40–€70).
- Day-long excursions, often paired with stops at nearby fjords (€100–€150).

What I Observed: On a late-afternoon cruise, the sun cast a golden light over the fjord, illuminating the waterfalls like liquid fire. The silence was broken only by the occasional call of a seagull, creating a moment of peace so profound it felt sacred.

Hiking Trails

For those who wish to connect more deeply with the landscape, Geirangerfjord's hiking trails offer a chance to see the fjord from above—and every step is rewarded with views that defy description.

1. Skageflå Farm Trail

Highlights: This steep but rewarding hike takes you to the Skageflå mountain farm, perched high above the fjord. The view of the Seven Sisters from this vantage point is unparalleled.

Duration: 2–4 hours round trip.

Tips: Wear sturdy, waterproof boots, as sections can be muddy.

What I Observed: As I stood on the edge of the cliff, overlooking the fjord far below, the world felt both vast and intimate at once. The sound of the waterfalls, carried up on the wind, added a musical backdrop that felt almost otherworldly.

2. Vesterås Ridge Trail

Highlights: This easier hike offers panoramic views of the fjord and its surrounding peaks. Perfect for families or those seeking a less strenuous option.

Duration: 1–2 hours.

Cultural and Historical Highlights

Geirangerfjord is not only a natural wonder but also a place deeply rooted in Norwegian history and culture.

The Geirangerfjord Heritage Center

Why Visit: This small museum offers fascinating insights into the fjord's geology, ecology, and human history. You'll learn about the daring farmers who lived on the cliffs and the role of the fjord as a vital trade route.
Price: €10–€15 entry.
What I Learned: Standing before a scale model of the fjord, I was struck by the ingenuity of the cliff farmers, who used ladders and ropes to move between their homes and the water below. Their resilience in the face of nature's challenges left me deeply humbled.

Fjord Farms
Scattered along the cliffs are abandoned farmsteads, some of which you can visit. These farms tell the story of a time when life here was not only beautiful but also incredibly demanding.
Observation: Seeing the remnants of these farms reminded me of how humans and nature have coexisted here for centuries, each shaped by the other.

Practical Tips and Observations
Weather
The weather in Geirangerfjord is as unpredictable as it is dramatic. Sunny mornings can give way to misty rain by afternoon, so pack layers and waterproof gear. Summer temperatures range from 10–20°C (50–68°F), while spring and autumn bring cooler but equally enchanting weather.

Wildlife
What to Look For:
- White-tailed eagles soaring above the cliffs.
- Seals and porpoises gliding through the water.
- Otters and, occasionally, deer near the shoreline.

What I Observed: During a quiet moment on the fjord, I spotted a white-tailed eagle perched high on a crag, scanning the waters below. Its presence, both regal and wild, felt like the embodiment of the fjord itself.

Dining and Staying in Geiranger
Dining
Local Specialties:
- Freshly caught salmon and trout.
- Norwegian waffles served with jam and sour cream.
- Brunost (brown cheese), a local delicacy with a sweet, caramelized flavor.

Where to Eat:
- Brasserie Posten: Known for its seasonal menus and fjord views (€20–€40 per meal).
- Fjordsight Café: A cozy spot for coffee and waffles (€10–€15).

Accommodation
Geiranger offers a range of options, from cozy cabins to luxury hotels.
Budget: Geiranger Camping (€30–€50 per night for tent pitches).
Mid-Range: Hotel Union Geiranger (€150–€250 per night).
Luxury: Havila Hotel Geiranger, with stunning fjord views (€300–€500 per night).

Nærøyfjord: UNESCO-protected beauty

There are places in this world that seem almost too beautiful to belong to reality, and Nærøyfjord is one of them. A narrow, mysterious gem cradled within Norway's fjordlands, this UNESCO World Heritage Site isn't just a location—it's a feeling. It's the sense of being enveloped by nature's grandeur, of existing in a space where time slows, and the world reclaims its quiet, awe-inspiring rhythm.

Nærøyfjord, an arm of the Sognefjord (Norway's longest fjord), stands as one of the narrowest and most dramatic fjords in the world. It feels untouched and sacred, as though it was forged by the hands of giants. Let me share with you every facet of this extraordinary destination—the places you must see, the ways you can experience it, and the indescribable emotions it evokes. Along the way, I'll sprinkle in personal moments that forever tethered my heart to this place.

The Journey into Nærøyfjord: A Passage Between Worlds

As you approach Nærøyfjord by boat or road, you'll notice the way the towering cliffs begin to close in. The fjord, just 250 meters wide at its narrowest point, feels like a natural cathedral. The walls soar 1,800 meters above the water, creating an almost vertical embrace that shuts out the outside world.

The stillness is profound, broken only by the occasional cry of a bird or the soft echo of waterfalls cascading down the cliffs. The water—so calm that it mirrors the cliffs above—adds to the surreal beauty. It feels like stepping into a painting where every detail has been lovingly rendered.

The Iconic Landmarks: Nature's Masterpieces

1. The Waterfalls

Nærøyfjord is alive with waterfalls, each a gleaming thread against the dark cliffs. The most iconic include:

- Sagfossen Waterfall: Tumbling dramatically down the cliffside, its roar can be heard even from afar.
- Rimstigen Waterfall: Often shrouded in mist, it feels like a veil drawn between the fjord and the heavens.

What I Observed: As the boat glided past Sagfossen, I leaned over the railing and felt the mist kiss my cheeks. It was more than just a visual wonder—it was tactile, a reminder of the raw, untamed power of nature.

2. The Cliffs and Caves
The vertical rock faces are streaked with colors—grays, browns, and greens—each telling a story of ancient glaciers and geological shifts. Look closely, and you'll find caves hidden among the cliffs, some of which are believed to have been shelters for Viking seafarers.

Ways to Experience Nærøyfjord: Adventure and Serenity
Nærøyfjord offers something for every traveler, whether you crave action or tranquility.

Fjord Cruises
Why It's Essential: A fjord cruise is the quintessential way to experience Nærøyfjord. The water's serenity contrasts with the dramatic cliffs, offering a unique perspective.
Options and Pricing:
- Classic sightseeing cruises (2 hours, €40–€70).
- Eco-friendly electric boats with silent engines that let you feel immersed in nature (€50–€80).
- Kayak excursions for a more intimate encounter with the water (€70–€100).

My Experience: I embarked on an early-morning cruise, the mist still clinging to the cliffs. As the boat rounded a bend, the sun pierced through, illuminating the fjord like a scene from a dream. I remember thinking that no photo could ever do this moment justice.

Hiking Trails

1. Rimstigen Trail
Highlights: This challenging hike rewards you with a bird's-eye view of the fjord. The climb is steep but offers unparalleled vistas from above.
Duration: 3–5 hours round trip.
What to Expect: Wildflowers dot the trail in spring, while autumn paints the landscape in hues of gold and crimson.

2. Bakkanosi Trail
Highlights: Starting from the small village of Bakka, this trail leads to a panoramic viewpoint where Nærøyfjord stretches out like a ribbon below.
Duration: 6–8 hours round trip.
Personal Tip: Pack a picnic and savor it at the summit—you'll never forget the combination of breathtaking views and simple food.

Wildlife: Nature's Residents
Nærøyfjord is teeming with life, from the water's depths to the skies above.

Marine Life: Spot seals lounging on rocky outcrops or porpoises playfully surfacing in the fjord's clear waters.
Birds: White-tailed eagles often glide gracefully above the cliffs, their sharp cries echoing in the stillness. Seabirds like cormorants and puffins are also common.
What I Saw: On a kayak trip, I had the privilege of watching a porpoise leap into the air, its sleek form catching the light. For a moment, it felt like the fjord itself had come alive to greet us.

Cultural and Historical Connections
The Village of Gudvangen

At the fjord's southern end lies the quaint village of Gudvangen, steeped in Viking history. It's a gateway to the fjord and home to:
Njardarheimr Viking Village: An immersive experience where you can learn about Viking life, try your hand at axe throwing, or enjoy traditional Viking food (€20–€30 entry).
Observation: Wandering through the reconstructed village, I felt a strange connection to the past, as though the stories of Viking explorers still whispered through the valley.

Fjord Farms

Scattered along the cliffs are old, abandoned farmsteads—remnants of a time when life here was both beautiful and harsh. Some are accessible by foot, offering a glimpse into the resilience of those who lived in harmony with this dramatic landscape.

Practical Tips for Visiting Nærøyfjord
When to Go
- Summer (June-August): Warm, long days perfect for cruises and hikes. Expect more visitors but also lush greenery.
- Spring (April-May): Waterfalls are at their fullest, and wildflowers bloom along the cliffs.
- Autumn (September-October): A quieter season with stunning fall colors.
- Winter (November-March): Snow adds a touch of magic, and the fjord feels incredibly serene. Ideal for Northern Lights chasers.

What to Wear

Dress in layers, as the weather can change rapidly. A waterproof jacket and sturdy hiking boots are must-haves.

Getting There
- By Boat: Many fjord cruises depart from Flåm or Gudvangen.
- By Car: Drive the E16 and take the winding road down to Gudvangen for an unforgettable journey.

Hardangerfjord: The orchard of Norway

In the heart of Norway's fjordlands lies a place so enchanting, so filled with life and beauty, that it seems as though it was designed to inspire poetry and dreams. Hardangerfjord, often called "The Orchard of Norway," is a region where nature and tradition intertwine in a harmonious dance. This fjord doesn't just amaze with its breathtaking landscapes—it seduces with its charm, its flavors, and its deep sense of history.

From the first blush of spring blossoms to the golden hues of autumn, Hardangerfjord's landscapes change with the seasons, but its magic remains timeless. Let me take you on a journey through this remarkable fjord, filled with detailed descriptions, personal reflections, and all the essential information to help you experience its beauty to the fullest.

A Fjord Like No Other: First Impressions

Hardangerfjord stretches for 179 kilometers, making it Norway's second-longest fjord. Its waters cut deeply into the rugged landscapes, creating a canvas of sheer cliffs, lush green valleys, and shimmering glaciers. But what sets Hardangerfjord apart is its sense of warmth—a feeling of life bursting forth in every corner.

As you enter Hardangerfjord, especially in the spring or summer, you'll be greeted by a spectacle that feels almost surreal. Orchards of cherry, apple, and pear trees line the fjord's shores, their blossoms creating an ocean of white and pink against the deep blue of the water. In autumn, these orchards give way to rows of fruit-laden trees, their boughs heavy with apples that seem almost too perfect to be real.

What I Felt: My first glimpse of Hardangerfjord left me speechless. The stillness of the fjord mirrored the cliffs above, doubling the beauty of the scene. The sweet scent of blossoms mingled with the crisp, salty air, creating a sensory experience I will never forget.

Exploring the Orchard of Norway: Highlights and Must-Sees

1. The Blossoming Orchards

What to Expect:

Each spring, Hardangerfjord transforms into a floral wonderland as millions of cherry and apple trees bloom. The orchards extend as far as the eye can see, covering the valley floors and climbing the surrounding hills.

The best time to visit is late April to mid-May, when the blossoms are at their peak.

What I Observed:

Walking through these orchards during the blooming season felt like stepping into a painting. The petals fluttered to the ground like snowflakes, carpeting the trails in soft whites and pinks. The hum of bees working tirelessly in the blossoms added a symphony of life to the tranquility.

2. Folgefonna Glacier

Why Visit:

This massive glacier, visible from parts of the fjord, offers a stark contrast to the lush valleys below. You can hike on the glacier, explore nearby ice caves, or simply marvel at its icy brilliance.

Guided glacier hikes start from €80–€120 per person and often include equipment.

What I Felt:

Standing on the glacier, I was struck by the raw power of nature. The air was sharp and cold, but the view of the fjord far below, framed by jagged ice formations, was worth every shiver.

3. Vøringsfossen Waterfall
Why Visit:
One of Norway's most iconic waterfalls, Vøringsfossen plummets 182 meters into a gorge below. A series of viewpoints and footbridges allow you to experience its power from multiple angles.
Entry is free, but guided tours are available for €30–€50.
What I Observed:
As I stood on a suspension bridge with the falls roaring beneath me, the mist rose and kissed my face. It was overwhelming in the best way possible—nature's raw energy on full display.

4. Trolltunga (The Troll's Tongue)
Why Visit:
One of Norway's most famous hikes, Trolltunga offers a dramatic view of Hardangerfjord from a cliff that juts out like a tongue into the abyss.
The hike is challenging (10–12 hours round trip), but the reward is one of the most photographed views in all of Norway.
Tips:
Be prepared with sturdy boots, plenty of water, and snacks. Guided hikes (€100–€150) are recommended for beginners.
What I Felt:
Sitting on the edge of Trolltunga with the fjord stretching endlessly below, I felt invincible yet insignificant at the same time—a strange and beautiful paradox.

Cultural and Culinary Highlights
Cider Culture
Hardangerfjord is known for its traditional apple cider, made from the fruit of the surrounding orchards. Visiting a cider house is a must, where you can taste everything from sparkling ciders to sweet dessert varieties.
Top Spots:
- Aga Sideri: Tours and tastings from €30–€50.
- Hardanger Saftog Siderfabrikk: Family-run with award-winning ciders.

What I Experienced: Sipping a glass of crisp cider on a sunny terrace overlooking the fjord was pure joy. Each sip carried the essence of the orchards—a perfect blend of sweetness and tartness.

Hardanger Fiddle and Folk Music
The Hardanger fiddle, a unique string instrument native to the region, produces a haunting, ethereal sound. Attend a local performance to experience traditional Norwegian folk music.
Where to Experience:
Hardanger Folkemuseum, entry €10–€15.

Practical Tips for Visiting Hardangerfjord
When to Visit
- Spring (April-May): Blossoms transform the fjord into a dreamscape.
- Summer (June-August): Perfect for hiking, kayaking, and enjoying warm days.
- Autumn (September-October): Harvest season brings a golden glow to the orchards.

- Winter (November-March): Snow blankets the fjord, creating a serene, magical atmosphere.

Getting Around
- By Car: Driving the Hardanger National Tourist Route is an experience in itself, with numerous viewpoints and picnic spots along the way.
- By Ferry: Scenic ferries operate between the fjord's villages, offering breathtaking views (€30–€50 for passengers).

Where to Stay
- Budget: Hardanger Hostel B&B (€70–€100 per night).
- Mid-Range: Hardanger Fjord Lodge (€150–€200 per night).
- Luxury: Hotel Ullensvang (€250–€400 per night), complete with an infinity pool overlooking the fjord.

Sognefjord: The king of fjords

Imagine a place where the grandeur of nature is so staggering, so humbling, that it feels like stepping into a timeless masterpiece. Sognefjord is exactly that place. Often called "The King of Fjords," this legendary stretch of water is the longest and deepest fjord in Norway—and a crown jewel of the Norwegian landscape. At 204 kilometers long and plunging to depths of 1,308 meters, Sognefjord isn't just a destination; it's an experience that demands to be felt with all your senses.

An Entrance Fit for a King

The first time I saw Sognefjord, it was as if the world had cracked open to reveal its most magnificent secret. The fjord stretched endlessly before me, framed by towering cliffs that seemed to rise from the water like ancient sentinels. The sheer size and scale of it are impossible to capture in words—it's something you feel in your chest, an awe that roots you to the spot.

The fjord's waters are a deep, almost hypnotic blue. On calm days, they mirror the cliffs and skies so perfectly that it feels like sailing through a dream. And when the light shifts—as it so often does in Norway—it paints the landscape in hues of gold, silver, and green, a constantly changing canvas that leaves you spellbound.

Why Sognefjord is the King of Fjords

Sognefjord owes its regal title to its sheer size and diversity. It branches into a series of narrow arms, each with its own unique charm and attractions. Here are the highlights you cannot miss:

1. Nærøyfjord: A UNESCO World Heritage Site
Why Visit: As one of Sognefjord's most dramatic arms, Nærøyfjord offers narrow passageways flanked by cliffs that soar up to 1,800 meters. It's nature at its most awe-inspiring.

Activities:
- Take a fjord cruise (prices range from €40–€80).
- Go kayaking for a more intimate exploration (€70–€100).
- Hike the Rimstigen Trail for panoramic views (3–5 hours round trip).

Personal Observation: Floating silently through Nærøyfjord, I found myself overwhelmed by the stillness. The cliffs seemed to hold their breath, creating an atmosphere of reverence. It was like being in a cathedral built by nature itself.

2. Fjærlandsfjord: Gateway to Glaciers

Why Visit: This arm of Sognefjord is home to two of Norway's most spectacular glaciers, the Jostedalsbreen and its arm, Bøyabreen.

Activities:
- Visit the Norwegian Glacier Museum (€15 entry).
- Take a guided glacier hike (€80–€120).

What to Observe: The glaciers shimmer under the sunlight, their icy blues contrasting sharply with the lush greenery of the valleys. Standing at the edge of Bøyabreen, you can hear the faint creaks and groans of the ancient ice—nature's quiet reminder of its power.

3. Lustrafjord: The Emerald Beauty

Why Visit: Known for its green-tinted waters (thanks to glacial runoff), Lustrafjord is a serene escape that feels almost otherworldly.

Activities:
- Visit Feigefossen, one of Norway's tallest waterfalls (218 meters).
- Explore the UNESCO-listed Urnes Stave Church, a wooden masterpiece dating back to the 12th century (€10–€15 entry).

Personal Reflection: At Feigefossen, I felt the mist from the waterfall on my face as sunlight refracted through the droplets, creating a rainbow. It was one of those moments where beauty feels almost physical—a weight in your chest, a lump in your throat.

Adventures Fit for Every Kind of Traveler

Sognefjord offers a wealth of activities, from serene cruises to adrenaline-fueled hikes. Here are some must-dos:

Fjord Cruises

Why It's a Must: To truly appreciate the scale of Sognefjord, you have to experience it from the water. Cruises range from short sightseeing trips to multi-hour journeys that weave through its arms.

Prices: €50–€150, depending on duration and inclusions.

Observation: On my cruise through the fjord, I remember being struck by the play of light on the water. The reflections of the cliffs turned the surface into a living painting, shifting and rippling with every breeze.

Hiking

1. Aurlandsdalen Valley:
Known as Norway's Grand Canyon, this trail offers dramatic views, cascading waterfalls, and lush meadows.
Duration: 1–2 days (various sections available).
Tip: Pack layers—it can be windy at higher altitudes.

2. Molden Hike:
A moderately challenging hike that rewards you with sweeping views over Lustrafjord.
Duration: 3–4 hours round trip.
What I Observed: Reaching the summit, I felt the wind whip around me as the fjord stretched out below, a shimmering ribbon of blue and green.

3. Kayaking:
Why It's Special: Gliding silently through the fjord allows you to connect with the landscape in a way that feels deeply personal.
Price Range: €70–€100 for guided tours.

Cultural and Historical Highlights

Sognefjord isn't just about natural beauty—it's steeped in history and culture, offering a glimpse into Norway's past.

Urnes Stave Church
As the oldest stave church in Norway, Urnes is a UNESCO World Heritage Site and a testament to medieval craftsmanship. Its intricate wooden carvings blend Norse mythology with Christian symbolism.
Entry Fee: €10–€15.
What I Felt: Sitting inside the church, surrounded by the scent of ancient wood, I felt a profound sense of connection to the generations who had worshipped here.

Local Villages
- Flåm: Famous for the Flåm Railway (€60–€70), one of the world's most scenic train journeys.
- Balestrand: A charming artist's village with galleries, traditional architecture, and breathtaking fjord views.

Wildlife: The King's Subjects
Sognefjord is alive with wildlife that adds to its majesty.

What to Look For:
- White-tailed eagles soaring above the cliffs.
- Seals basking on rocky outcrops.
- Porpoises occasionally surfacing in the fjord's waters.

Personal Moment: On a quiet morning, I watched a family of seals lounging near a secluded shore. Their playful interactions brought a sense of joy and vitality to the fjord's peaceful expanse.

Practical Information
When to Visit
- Summer (June-August): Warm weather and endless daylight make this the best time for outdoor activities.
- Spring (April-May): Waterfalls are at their most powerful, and wildflowers bloom along the fjord.

- Autumn (September-October): Fewer crowds and stunning fall colors.
- Winter (November-March): A serene, snow-covered wonderland.

Where to Stay
- Budget: Vangsgaarden Gjestgiveri (€80–€120 per night).
- Mid-Range: Fretheim Hotel in Flåm (€150–€200 per night).
- **Luxury**: Kviknes Hotel in Balestrand (€250–€400 per night).

Final Thoughts

Sognefjord isn't just the King of Fjords—it's a place that reminds you of the majesty of the natural world. It's the way the cliffs rise like ancient guardians, the way the water reflects the sky as if trying to hold onto it, and the way every corner of the fjord invites you to stop, breathe, and simply be.

Visiting Sognefjord isn't just a trip—it's a return to something essential, something primal. It's a chance to stand in the presence of greatness and feel the profound joy of being alive. So come, let the King of Fjords welcome you into its realm. You'll leave not as a visitor, but as someone forever changed.

Chapter 6: Ports of Call

Bergen: The cultural heart of the Fjords

Nestled between seven mountains and kissed by the waters of seven fjords, Bergen is more than just a city—it is a symphony of culture, history, and natural beauty. As the gateway to the Norwegian Fjords, Bergen pulses with life, a vibrant crossroads where past meets present. Every street, every house, every salty breath of air whispers stories of its seafaring heritage and artistic soul.

Bryggen: Where History Lives

Bryggen, Bergen's iconic wharf, is a kaleidoscope of colorful wooden buildings lining the harbor. These structures, with their weathered facades and slanted roofs, have stood the test of time since the Hanseatic League made Bergen a key trading hub in the 14th century. Today, Bryggen is not just a place—it's an experience.

What to Explore
Bryggen Museum:
This museum unveils the secrets of medieval Bergen through artifacts unearthed during archaeological digs.
Entry Fee: €10–€15.
What to Observe: Touch the timbers of the original foundations, darkened by age and glowing with history. The smell of wood and earth feels like stepping into another century.

Shops and Galleries:
Wander through boutiques selling handmade ceramics, woven textiles, and jewelry inspired by Viking designs.
Personal Observation: In a tiny workshop, I watched an artisan carve intricate patterns into a silver pendant. She smiled as she explained how each design carried a story, a legacy of Bergen's past.

UNESCO Recognition:

Bryggen's status as a UNESCO World Heritage Site ensures its preservation. Every warped beam and narrow alley feels alive with the whispers of traders who once bustled through its corridors.

The Fløibanen Funicular and Mount Fløyen

For a bird's-eye view of Bergen, the Fløibanen Funicular is an unmissable adventure. This scenic railway whisks you from the heart of the city to the summit of Mount Fløyen in under 10 minutes.

Practical Details
Cost: €15–€20 round trip.
What to Observe:
- As the funicular ascends, the city unfolds like a living map: terracotta rooftops give way to sparkling fjords and endless horizons.
- At the summit, Mount Fløyen offers hiking trails, picnic spots, and playful goats that delight visitors of all ages.

What I Felt: Standing at the viewpoint, the crisp mountain air filled my lungs as the city lay serenely below. I watched boats crisscross the harbor, their wakes trailing like fleeting memories. It was as though the entire world paused, just for that moment.

Local Cuisine: A Taste of the Sea

Bergen's culinary scene reflects its maritime heritage. The city is a haven for seafood lovers, with flavors as fresh and vibrant as the fjords themselves.

Where to Eat
Fish Market (Fisketorget):
A lively hub where vendors showcase everything from salmon and shrimp to reindeer sausage.
What to Try:
- Grilled stockfish with a side of creamy potatoes (€15–€30).
- King crab legs, their sweetness elevated with a dash of lemon.

Personal Experience: I savored a bowl of Bergen fish soup, its creamy broth bursting with the flavors of cod, carrots, and a hint of dill. Sitting at a market table with seagulls wheeling above, I felt utterly immersed in Bergen's rhythm.

Cornelius Seafood Restaurant:
Located on a private island accessible by boat, this restaurant offers a dining experience as unforgettable as its views.
Price Range: €100–€200 for a multi-course meal.
What to Observe: The open kitchen invites you to watch chefs transform the day's catch into edible masterpieces.

The Arts and Culture of Bergen

Bergen is a city that thrives on creativity. From its music to its festivals, every corner brims with artistic energy.

Bergen International Festival
Why It's Special:

Held every spring, this festival is a celebration of music, theater, and dance, attracting artists from around the globe.
Ticket Prices: €20–€150, depending on the event.
Personal Experience: I attended a concert in Grieghallen, where the haunting strains of a violin seemed to echo the melancholy beauty of the fjords. The music lingered in my soul, long after the applause faded.

Street Art
Bergen's walls are alive with colorful murals and graffiti, showcasing the city's contemporary creative spirit.
What to Look For: Explore Skostredet, a charming street filled with quirky shops and vibrant street art.

Bergen's Connection to the Fjords
As the gateway to the Norwegian Fjords, Bergen offers countless opportunities to venture into the surrounding landscapes.

Norway in a Nutshell Tour
Why It's Popular:
This famous tour combines scenic train rides, boat cruises, and bus journeys to showcase the best of the fjords.
Price: €150–€300, depending on the itinerary.
Highlights:
Cruise through Nærøyfjord, a UNESCO World Heritage Site.
Ride the Flåm Railway, one of the world's most beautiful train journeys.

Hiking Around Bergen
Mount Ulriken: The highest of Bergen's seven mountains, offering challenging trails and unbeatable views. The Ulriken Cable Car (€20–€30) provides an easy way to reach the summit.
Personal Observation: On a hike near Mount Ulriken, I paused to drink from a stream that trickled down the slope. The water was icy, pure, and tasted of the earth—a reminder of the untouched beauty that surrounds Bergen.

Practical Tips for Visiting Bergen

When to Visit
- Summer (June-August): The warmest weather and endless daylight make this the ideal time to explore.
- Spring (April-May): Experience Bergen's cherry blossoms and the International Festival.
- Autumn (September-October): Crisp air and fewer crowds offer a quieter charm.
- Winter (November-March): Bergen's snow-dusted rooftops and cozy cafes create a magical, intimate atmosphere.

Getting Around
Bergen Card:
Offers free or discounted entry to attractions, as well as unlimited public transport (€30–€50 for 24–72 hours).

Tip: Use the card to explore Bergen's museums, including the KODE Art Museums and Composer Homes.

Where to Stay
- Budget: Marken Guesthouse (€40–€80 per night).
- Mid-Range: Magic Hotel Solheimsviken (€120–€180 per night).
- Luxury: Opus XVI, a boutique hotel inspired by Edvard Grieg (€250–€400 per night).

Ålesund: Art Nouveau architecture and adventure

If ever there was a city that could be described as a living, breathing work of art, Ålesund is it. Situated on Norway's western coast, this gem stretches across multiple islands connected by bridges, giving it a dreamy, maritime atmosphere. But what truly sets Ålesund apart is its striking Art Nouveau architecture—a unique result of tragedy and triumph. It's a place where ornate towers, pastel-colored facades, and intricate designs meet the rugged beauty of fjords and mountains. And yet, beneath this beauty lies a spirit of adventure that invites you to explore its winding streets and surrounding wilderness.

A City Reborn: The Story Behind the Art Nouveau Marvel

In 1904, a devastating fire swept through Ålesund, reducing most of the wooden city to ashes. Nearly 850 houses were destroyed, and thousands were left homeless. But out of the ashes rose something extraordinary. The city was rebuilt in the Art Nouveau style, also known as Jugendstil, by architects and craftsmen who infused every corner with creativity and elegance.

Today, Ålesund stands as one of the world's best-preserved examples of Art Nouveau architecture, a rare and captivating legacy born from resilience.

Art Nouveau Architecture: A Living Fairy Tale

Walking through Ålesund is like stepping into a storybook. The narrow streets are lined with buildings adorned with curved lines, floral motifs, and whimsical turrets. Each facade tells its own story, and the more you explore, the more intricate details you discover.

What to See
Jugendstilsenteret (Art Nouveau Centre): Located in a former pharmacy, this museum offers an interactive look at Ålesund's transformation after the fire. You'll learn about

the architects who shaped the city and see original blueprints, furnishings, and exhibits.
Price: €10–€15.
What to Observe: The stained glass windows and carved details, which feel like a time capsule of early 20th-century design.
Personal Reflection: Walking through the museum felt like tracing the fingerprints of history. Each design choice, each curve and flourish, spoke of a city determined to rebuild not just its homes but its identity.

Pedestrian Streets of Kongens Gate and Apotekergata:
These vibrant streets are where Art Nouveau architecture truly shines. Look up to see dragon motifs, floral designs, and fantastical gargoyles.
What I Observed: I found myself stopping constantly to admire the buildings—some painted in soft pastels, others in bold reds and yellows. It felt like walking through a city built for dreamers.

The View from Mount Aksla: Ålesund's Crown Jewel

For a breathtaking perspective of Ålesund, a visit to Mount Aksla is a must. The climb (or bus ride) rewards you with a panoramic view of the city, the surrounding islands, and the sparkling fjords beyond.

How to Get There
- By Foot: Climb the 418 steps from the town park. The steps are well-maintained, and there are benches along the way for resting.
- By Car or Bus: For a more relaxed ascent, buses and taxis can take you to the viewpoint.

Cost: Free to climb; buses range from €5–€10.

What to Expect
At the summit, Fjellstua Café awaits, where you can enjoy coffee or a light meal while soaking in the view.
What I Observed: From the top, Ålesund unfolds like a postcard. The Art Nouveau buildings shimmer in the sunlight, the fjords stretch out like liquid silver, and the surrounding mountains seem to embrace the city in their quiet majesty. I remember feeling so small yet so connected to the world around me.

Adventure Beyond the City: Fjords, Islands, and Wildlife

While Ålesund's architecture captivates, its surroundings beckon with adventures that are equally unforgettable. Whether you're exploring the fjords, hiking rugged trails, or spotting puffins, there's something here for every nature lover.

Explore Hjørundfjord
Often called a hidden gem, Hjørundfjord is a 35-kilometer fjord framed by towering peaks. It's quieter than the more famous fjords, offering an experience that feels deeply personal.
Activities:
- Fjord cruises (€50–€100).
- Hiking in the Sunnmøre Alps, known for their dramatic landscapes.

Personal Reflection: On a small boat cruising through Hjørundfjord, I marveled at waterfalls cascading down the cliffs and the occasional mountain farm perched impossibly high. It felt like a scene plucked straight from a fantasy novel.

Island-Hopping Adventure
Ålesund's position on multiple islands makes it an ideal base for exploring nearby gems like Runde and Godøy.

Runde Island:
Known as Norway's "Bird Island," Runde is home to over 500,000 seabirds, including puffins, guillemots, and razorbills.
What to Do: Take a guided boat tour (€40–€70) to see the bird colonies up close, or hike the island's trails for sweeping ocean views.
What I Observed: Watching puffins waddle along the cliffs and dive into the water with almost comical determination was pure joy. Their presence added a playful energy to the island's rugged beauty.

Alnes Lighthouse on Godøy Island:
This historic lighthouse, still operational, offers stunning views of the Atlantic Ocean. The nearby beach is perfect for quiet reflection.
Entry Fee: €5–€10.

Local Cuisine: A Taste of Coastal Norway

Ålesund's food scene is rooted in its coastal location, with fresh seafood taking center stage. From charming cafes to fine dining, there's something to satisfy every palate.

Where to Eat
XL Diner:
Famous for its bacalao (traditional Norwegian cod stew) and stunning harbor views.
Price Range: €30–€50.
What to Observe: The delicate balance of flavors in the bacalao—a symphony of tangy, savory, and sweet.

Brokost Café:
A cozy spot for coffee and pastries, perfect for a morning break.
What to Try: Traditional cinnamon buns (€5–€8).

Practical Tips for Visiting Ålesund
When to Visit
- Summer (June-August): Long days and mild weather make this the best time for exploring.
- Spring (April-May): Fewer crowds and blooming flowers add charm.

- Autumn (September-October): A quieter season with vibrant fall colors.
- Winter (November-March): Snow adds a magical touch to the city, and cozy cafes offer respite from the cold.

Getting Around
- Ålesund is highly walkable, with most attractions clustered in the city center. For longer trips, buses and ferries are convenient.
- Bicycle Rentals: A fun way to explore the islands (€15–€30 per day).

Where to Stay
- Budget: Ålesund Hostel (€40–€80 per night).
- Mid-Range: Hotel Brosundet (€150–€200 per night), housed in a converted warehouse with stunning fjord views.
- Luxury: Hotel Storfjord (€250–€400 per night), offering secluded elegance surrounded by nature.

Stavanger: A mix of history and nature

Stavanger—a city that elegantly wears two faces, each as captivating as the other. On one side, it tells the story of Norway's storied past, a tale of Vikings, centuries-old architecture, and maritime significance. On the other, it offers a gateway to some of the country's most breathtaking natural wonders, from dramatic cliffs to serene fjords. To visit Stavanger is to step into a world where history and nature dance together in perfect harmony, creating a destination that feels both grounded and endlessly adventurous..

Old Stavanger: A Step Back in Time

As you wander through Old Stavanger (Gamle Stavanger), it's impossible not to feel as though you've been transported to another era. This historic district, home to Europe's best-preserved collection of wooden houses, exudes charm from every corner. The cobblestone streets wind between 18th and 19th-century homes, all painted in pristine white, with windowsills adorned with flower pots and lace curtains swaying in the gentle breeze.

What to Explore
Preservation Marvel:
Over 170 wooden houses stand here, meticulously preserved as a reminder of Stavanger's maritime heritage. Walking these streets feels like stepping into a living museum.

Personal Reflection: As I strolled past these homes, I couldn't help but imagine the lives of the sailors, merchants, and artisans who once lived here. There was a warmth to the air, as though the walls themselves held the laughter and dreams of generations past.

Norwegian Canning Museum:
Located in a former cannery, this museum offers an intimate glimpse into Stavanger's role in the sardine industry. The sights, smells, and sounds of the factory are recreated with stunning detail.
Entry Fee: €10–€15.
What to Observe: The vintage machinery and historical photos create a vivid picture of Stavanger's industrial past. I'll never forget the satisfying sizzle of the sardines being packed during the live demonstration.

The Stavanger Cathedral: A Masterpiece of Faith and Architecture
Dominating the heart of Stavanger is its magnificent cathedral, Domkirken. Built in the 12th century, it's the oldest cathedral in Norway that has remained in continuous use. Its Gothic arches, intricate stone carvings, and medieval atmosphere make it a must-see.

What to Observe

- Stained Glass Windows: The light streaming through these beautifully crafted windows bathes the interior in a warm glow, creating an almost sacred ambiance.
- Stone Details: The intricate carvings of biblical scenes and mythical creatures are a testament to the craftsmanship of the time.
- Organ Concerts: If you're fortunate, catch an organ recital. The acoustics are breathtaking, turning music into a transcendent experience.

Entry Fee: €5–€10.

What I Felt: Sitting in a wooden pew, the quiet hum of the cathedral surrounded me. The air was thick with history—a thousand years of prayer, hope, and resilience reverberating in the stone walls.

Nature's Masterpiece: Preikestolen (Pulpit Rock)
While Stavanger's historical allure is undeniable, its true showstopper lies just beyond the city—a towering cliff known as Preikestolen, or Pulpit Rock. This 604-meter-high plateau juts dramatically over Lysefjord, offering one of the most iconic views in Norway.

The Hike to Preikestolen
- Duration: 4–6 hours round trip.
- Difficulty: Moderate, with rocky paths and some steep sections.
- Guided Tours: €80–€150, including transportation and a local guide.

What I Observed: The hike begins through a lush forest, where the scent of pine mingles with the earthy aroma of damp soil. As you ascend, the trees thin out, revealing glimpses of the fjord below. Upon reaching the summit, the reward is unparalleled: a sweeping panorama of blue-green waters flanked by jagged cliffs.

Tips for Visiting
- Timing: Start early to avoid crowds and enjoy the sunrise.
- What to Pack: Sturdy hiking boots, water, snacks, and a windproof jacket—Pulpit Rock is notorious for its sudden gusts.

Personal Reflection: Standing at the edge of Pulpit Rock, I felt the wind whip around me, a wild and exhilarating reminder of nature's power. Below, the fjord gleamed like polished glass, reflecting the cliffs and sky. It wasn't just a view; it was a moment of pure connection with the earth.

Kjeragbolten: An Adrenaline-Fueled Adventure

For those seeking an even greater thrill, Kjeragbolten awaits—a giant boulder wedged precariously between two cliffs, dangling 1,000 meters above Lysefjord.

The Experience
- Hike Duration: 6–10 hours round trip.
- Difficulty: Challenging, with steep inclines and rocky terrain.
- Photo Opportunity: If you're brave enough, step onto the boulder for a once-in-a-lifetime photo.

What I Observed: Balancing on Kjeragbolten is not for the faint of heart, but the sense of triumph that follows is incomparable. The adrenaline coursing through my veins, paired with the sheer beauty of the fjord below, left me feeling invincible.

Sverd i Fjell (Swords in Rock): A Tribute to Norway's Viking Past

Just outside Stavanger, three massive swords rise from the ground, their bronze blades reflecting Norway's Viking heritage. Known as Sverd i Fjell (Swords in Rock), this monument commemorates the Battle of Hafrsfjord, where

King Harald Fairhair united Norway into a single kingdom.

What to Observe
- Symbolism: Each sword represents peace, unity, and freedom.
- The Setting: Overlooking Hafrsfjord, the serene waters contrast beautifully with the monument's raw strength.

What I Felt: As I stood before these towering swords, the weight of history was palpable. It was a reminder of the sacrifices and victories that shaped Norway into the nation it is today.

Local Cuisine: Fresh from the Fjords

Stavanger's culinary scene reflects its coastal location, blending fresh seafood with modern innovation.

Where to Eat
Fisketorget (Fish Market):
- Try the grilled mackerel or fish cakes (€15–€30).
- Observation: The vendors are storytellers, eager to share the origins of their catch.

RE-NAA:
Stavanger's Michelin-starred restaurant, celebrated for its creative, seasonal menus.

Price: €150–€250 for a multi-course experience.

Practical Tips for Visiting Stavanger
Best Time to Visit
- Summer (June-August): Mild weather and long daylight hours make this the ideal season for outdoor adventures.
- Spring and Autumn (April-May, September-October): Cooler temperatures and fewer crowds offer a quieter charm.

Where to Stay
- Budget: Stavanger Bed & Breakfast (€50–€80 per night).
- Mid-Range: Scandic Stavanger City (€120–€180 per night).
- Luxury: Eilert Smith Hotel (€250–€400 per night).

Tromsø: The Arctic capital

Far above the Arctic Circle, where the world feels both raw and untamed, lies Tromsø—Norway's Arctic capital. It's a place that embodies the enchantment of the far north, offering a captivating blend of natural beauty, rich history, and a culture shaped by its connection to the Arctic wilderness. Tromsø is where the midnight sun dances endlessly in the summer sky, and the ethereal Northern Lights paint the winter nights in shades of green, purple, and gold. This city is not just a destination; it's an adventure, a feeling, and a memory waiting to be made.

First Impressions: A Gateway to the Arctic

Arriving in Tromsø feels like stepping into another world. The air is crisp, carrying with it a hint of snow or salt, depending on the season. The city is both lively and tranquil, with its vibrant harbor surrounded by majestic snow-draped mountains. Tromsø sits on Tromsøya, an island connected to the mainland by graceful bridges, and the waters of the fjord lap gently at its edges.

The first thing you'll notice about Tromsø is its light. Depending on when you visit, this Arctic city is bathed in either the 24-hour glow of the Midnight Sun or the soft, magical blue of Polar Night. These unique phenomena shape not just the environment but the very soul of the city.

The Northern Lights: Nature's Grandest Show

Tromsø is one of the best places in the world to witness the aurora borealis. When the skies come alive with dancing ribbons of light, it feels as though the universe is putting on a performance just for you.

Best Ways to Experience the Northern Lights

Guided Aurora Tours:
Local guides know the best spots to escape city light pollution and maximize your chances of seeing the lights.
Price Range: €100–€150 per person.
Personal Note: On a frosty winter night, I joined a small group tour to a remote fjord. Wrapped in thick blankets, we sipped hot chocolate as the aurora began its dance. The first glimpse of green light shimmering across the sky took my breath away—it was a moment of pure awe that words can't capture.

Northern Lights Cruises:
Set sail on the fjord for a unique vantage point, with the lights reflecting off the water. (€120–€200).

Aurora Camps:
Stay in heated "aurora huts" or Sami-inspired tents in the wilderness for an immersive experience. (€150–€300 per night).

Tips for Seeing the Lights
- When to Go: Late September to early April offers the best chances.

- What to Bring: Dress warmly in layers, bring a tripod for photography, and pack plenty of patience—nature's greatest spectacles can require waiting.

Summer's Midnight Sun: Endless Days of Light

While Tromsø is famous for its winter wonders, summer brings its own magic. From late May to late July, the Midnight Sun bathes the landscape in a golden light, creating a surreal atmosphere that inspires exploration.

What to Do in the Midnight Sun

Hiking Mount Storsteinen:
Take the Fjellheisen cable car (€20–€30) to the top of Mount Storsteinen, then hike further into the Lyngen Alps for breathtaking views.
What I Observed: The midnight sun turned the snow-capped peaks and fjords into a canvas of amber and gold. Time felt irrelevant, as though nature itself refused to sleep.

Kayaking Through the Fjords:
Paddle through crystal-clear waters surrounded by dramatic cliffs and wildlife (€70–€120).
Wildlife Safari:
Spot reindeer, whales, and Arctic foxes under the never-setting sun (€150–€200).

The Sami Culture: Stories of the Indigenous Arctic People

Tromsø is a gateway to experiencing the traditions and lifestyle of the Sami people, the Indigenous inhabitants of the Arctic region. Their connection to nature, storytelling, and reindeer herding offers a fascinating glimpse into a way of life shaped by the harsh beauty of the north.

Sami Experiences

Reindeer Sledding and Sami Storytelling:
Meet Sami guides, feed their reindeer, and hear ancient stories while sitting by a crackling fire (€100–€200).
What I Felt: On a snowy day, I held the reins of a reindeer sled as it glided through a pristine Arctic forest. Later, inside a warm lavvu (traditional tent), a Sami elder shared tales of the northern lights and the reindeer's sacred role in their culture. It was a rare and beautiful connection to a history intertwined with the land.

Sami Festivals:
Visit Tromsø during the Sami Week in February to witness joik singing, traditional dress, and reindeer races.

Tromsø's Cultural and Historical Treasures

While nature takes center stage in Tromsø, the city itself is rich in culture and history.

Arctic Cathedral (Ishavskatedralen)

This striking landmark, with its modern triangular design, reflects the surrounding mountains and icebergs. Inside, a massive stained-glass window adds a sense of wonder and serenity.
Entry Fee: €5–€10.
What to Observe: The way the sunlight filters through the stained glass, casting ethereal patterns on the walls.

Polar Museum

Discover Tromsø's history as a base for Arctic explorers, including stories of seal hunters and polar expeditions.
Entry Fee: €10–€15.

Personal Reflection: Holding replicas of Arctic tools, I marveled at the bravery and ingenuity it took to survive in such a harsh environment.

Tromsø University Museum
Learn about the northern lights, Sami culture, and Arctic flora and fauna at this engaging museum. (€10–€15).

Culinary Delights: Arctic-Inspired Flavors
Tromsø's dining scene reflects its Arctic surroundings, offering everything from fresh seafood to reindeer stew. The cuisine here is as adventurous as the landscape.

Where to Eat
- Mathallen Tromsø: A modern eatery with Arctic char, king crab, and gourmet reindeer dishes (€30–€50).
- Emma's Dream Kitchen: Cozy and creative, with excellent fish soup and locally sourced ingredients (€25–€40).

Personal Experience: At a waterside café, I savored a plate of smoked salmon while watching fishing boats glide into the harbor. The fish tasted so fresh, it felt like the fjord itself had gifted it to the table.

Practical Tips for Visiting Tromsø
Getting Around
Tromsø is walkable, but buses are convenient for exploring outer areas (€3–€5 per ride).

Airport Transfers: The city is just 10 minutes from Tromsø Airport (€10–€15 by shuttle).

When to Visit
- Winter (November-March): Northern Lights and snowy adventures.
- Summer (May-July): Midnight Sun and endless outdoor activities.

Where to Stay
- Budget: Smarthotel Tromsø (€80–€120 per night).
- Mid-Range: Thon Hotel Polar (€150–€200 per night).
- Luxury: Scandic Ishavshotel (€250–€400 per night), boasting stunning harbor views.

Final Thoughts
Tromsø is more than just a city—it's an Arctic symphony, a place where nature's wonders and human spirit collide in a breathtaking dance. It's the silence of watching the northern lights ripple across a star-drenched sky, the warmth of Sami stories told by firelight, and the thrill of hiking under a sun that never sets.

For me, Tromsø was a revelation. It reminded me of the vastness of the world and the beauty that exists even in its most remote corners. Whether you're standing on the edge of a fjord or sharing reindeer stew with a Sami guide, Tromsø invites you to feel alive in a way few places can.

Chapter 7: Shore Excursions and Activities

Hiking the trails of Norwegian legends

Have you ever walked a path that felt like it carried the weight of centuries? Have you ever climbed a trail where each step echoed with the whispers of myth and history, where the wind seemed to sing ancient songs of gods and giants, of daring Vikings and untamed nature? If not, then let me tell you: hiking the trails of Norwegian legends is an experience that will change you. These are not just hikes—they are journeys into the soul of Norway, where the breathtaking landscapes are woven together with stories as old as the mountains themselves.

When I set out to explore these legendary trails, I thought I knew what to expect—beautiful views, some physical challenge, perhaps a moment of quiet reflection. What I found, however, was something far greater. Each trail told its own story, revealing a piece of Norway's heart and stirring emotions I hadn't anticipated. Let me take you through these extraordinary hikes, and I promise that by the end, you'll be lacing up your boots and packing your sense of wonder.

<u>Preikestolen (Pulpit Rock): Standing on the Edge of Legend</u>

- Location: Lysefjord, near Stavanger.

- Distance and Difficulty: 8 kilometers round trip, moderate (4–5 hours).
- Cost: Free to hike; parking at the trailhead costs around €20.

Preikestolen, or Pulpit Rock, is one of Norway's most iconic hikes—a sheer cliff that rises 604 meters above the turquoise waters of Lysefjord. Legend has it that the gods themselves created this rock to serve as a pulpit from which to oversee the fjords and mountains. Standing there, I could almost feel their presence.

The trail begins with a steady climb through a forest. The scent of pine fills the air, and the sound of distant waterfalls creates a soothing rhythm. Soon, the forest gives way to open rock faces, where cairns mark the path and reveal glimpses of the fjord below. The final stretch is a scramble over boulders before the breathtaking vista unfolds.

What I Observed: As I stood at the edge of Preikestolen, the wind tugging at my jacket, the fjord stretched out endlessly below. The cliffs cast shadows over the water, and the light shifted, turning the fjord from deep green to shimmering silver. It felt as though time had paused to let me drink in the view. I remember a tiny flower growing in a crack in the rock, defiant and beautiful—a reminder of life's resilience in even the most precarious places.

Trolltunga (The Troll's Tongue): The Stuff of Norse Myth

- Location: Near Odda, Hardangerfjord.
- Distance and Difficulty: 28 kilometers round trip, challenging (10–12 hours).
- Cost: Free to hike; parking fees range from €30–€50.

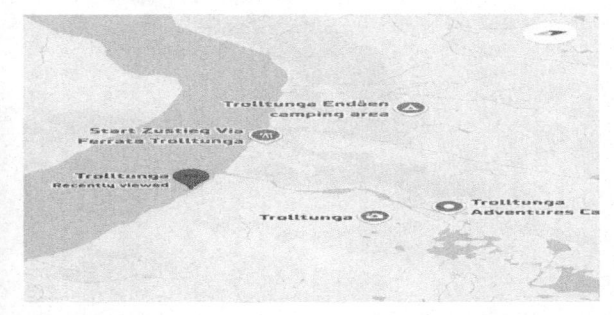

Trolltunga is no ordinary hike. It's a journey to a mythical realm, where a rock juts out 700 meters above Ringedalsvatnet Lake, resembling a troll's tongue—a symbol of defiance against the gods. According to legend, trolls gather here at night to laugh at the mortals below. Standing on Trolltunga, you feel as though you've stepped into their world.

The trail begins at Mågelitopp, winding through forests and across rivers. It's a grueling climb at times, with rocky inclines and marshy flats, but each step reveals a new layer of beauty. The reward? That iconic tongue of rock and a view that seems to stretch forever.

What I Observed: The moment I stepped onto Trolltunga, my legs ached from the climb, but my heart swelled with triumph. Below, the lake shimmered like liquid glass, reflecting the sky. The silence was broken only by the wind, carrying with it a sense of ancient power. As I gazed into the distance, I felt a strange mix of insignificance and invincibility—an intoxicating paradox.

Besseggen Ridge: Where Heroes Walked
- Location: Jotunheimen National Park, near Gjendesheim.
- Distance and Difficulty: 14 kilometers one way, strenuous (6–8 hours).
- Cost: Ferry to the trailhead costs €20–€30.

Besseggen is more than just a ridge; it's a path that feels like it belongs in a saga. The hike offers jaw-dropping views of Gjende and Bessvatnet—two lakes, one emerald green and the other deep blue, separated by a thin ridge. According to legend, Norse warriors walked this path to prove their courage.

The trail begins with a ferry ride across Gjende Lake to Memurubu. From there, the hike ascends steeply, with rocky switchbacks and exposed ridges. It's not for the faint-hearted, but the vistas are worth every drop of sweat.

What I Observed: Halfway along the ridge, I paused to catch my breath and drink some water. Below me, the two lakes glimmered like twin jewels, their colors impossibly vibrant. The clouds seemed close enough to touch, and the wind carried the faint scent of moss and stone. I remember seeing a lone raven perched on a rock, its black feathers gleaming in the sunlight—a figure of mystery and wisdom in this mythical landscape.

Romsdalseggen Ridge: A Symphony of Peaks and Valleys

- Location: Åndalsnes, Romsdal.
- Distance and Difficulty: 10 kilometers one way, moderate to challenging (5–7 hours).
- Cost: Shuttle bus to the trailhead costs around €20.

Romsdalseggen is a hike that feels like a symphony, with its sweeping views of the Romsdal Alps, the Rauma River, and the dramatic Trollveggen (Troll Wall). Legends say that the Trollveggen cliffs were the battleground of giants, their fiery clashes leaving behind the jagged peaks.

The trail winds through wildflower-strewn meadows and steep ridges. Each section feels like a new movement in a symphony, building towards the crescendo—the summit.

What I Observed: As I stood on Romsdalseggen, the peaks of the Troll Wall loomed like ancient guardians. The valleys below were a patchwork of green and gold, and the river snaked through them like a silver ribbon. The sunlight danced on the water, and I felt as though the earth itself was alive, humming with energy.

Why You Should Hike These Trails

these trails are not just about physical challenge or scenic beauty—they are gateways to another world, where legends come alive and nature reveals its raw, untamed power. Hiking them is like stepping into a story, where you become both the hero and the witness.

- For the Views: The landscapes are unparalleled, with fjords, cliffs, and lakes that defy imagination.
- For the History: Each trail carries the weight of Norwegian legends, connecting you to a rich cultural heritage.
- For the Soul: There's something profoundly healing about walking in these wild places, where the air is pure and the silence speaks volumes.

Kayaking through serene fjord waters

Kayaking through the fjords is more than just an activity; it's a journey into something primal and profound. It's an experience that stays with you long after your paddle has dipped for the last time. I've had the privilege of kayaking these waters, and it was nothing short of transformative. Allow me to take you through why you absolutely must do this, along with all the details you'll need to embark on your own fjord-kayaking adventure.

The Perfect Locations for Fjord Kayaking

Norway's fjords are numerous, each with its own unique character, beauty, and allure. Here are some of the most unforgettable kayaking destinations:

Nærøyfjord: A UNESCO World Heritage Gem

Location: An arm of the larger Sognefjord, near Flåm and Gudvangen.

Why It's Perfect for Kayaking: Narrow and dramatic, Nærøyfjord feels like a world frozen in time. Its cliffs soar 1,800 meters above the water, and its tranquil atmosphere is unmatched.

Experience:
Guided kayak tours start from Gudvangen, lasting between 2–4 hours (€70–€120). These trips often include stops to explore hidden waterfalls or learn about the fjord's history.

What I Observed: Paddling through Nærøyfjord was like gliding through a cathedral of nature. The silence was profound—so complete, I could hear the echoes of my paddle breaking the surface of the water. I remember spotting a lone goat perched on a narrow ledge, its gaze serene and unbothered by the world below.

Geirangerfjord: Beauty Crowned by Waterfalls

Location: Near the village of Geiranger, Central Norway.

Why It's Perfect for Kayaking: Known for its UNESCO-listed waterfalls like the Seven Sisters, this fjord offers unparalleled scenery paired with rich cultural heritage.

Experience:
Half-day guided kayak tours cost around €80–€100, while full-day options that include lunch breaks or stops for swimming are priced at €120–€150.

What I Observed: One afternoon, as I paddled near the Seven Sisters waterfalls, a rainbow arched over the misty spray. The water shimmered, catching fragments of color, and the cliffs loomed overhead, dripping with greenery. It felt like stepping into a fairytale.

Lysefjord: Preikestolen's Majestic Waters

Location: Near Stavanger, Southern Norway.
Why It's Perfect for Kayaking: The fjord is flanked by awe-inspiring rock formations, including the iconic Preikestolen (Pulpit Rock), which towers 604 meters above.
Experience:
Evening kayak tours, perfect for catching the fjord bathed in sunset hues, cost about €70–€90.
What I Observed: At dusk, the water turned an inky blue, mirroring the golden light spilling over the edges of Preikestolen. The quiet was broken only by the distant cry of a gull and the rhythmic dip of my paddle.

Hardangerfjord: The Orchard of Norway

Location: Near Odda, Western Norway.
Why It's Perfect for Kayaking: Surrounded by fruit orchards, cascading waterfalls, and the shimmering Folgefonna Glacier, Hardangerfjord is a sensory feast.
Experience:
Eco-friendly kayak rentals start at €50 for half a day, and guided tours cost €80–€120.
What I Observed: As I paddled past the small village of Lofthus, the scent of blooming apple orchards filled the air. The juxtaposition of the glacier's icy brilliance and the valley's verdant beauty was nothing short of poetic.

Why Kayaking the Fjords is Unforgettable

Unlike larger vessels, kayaks allow you to navigate narrow passages, get close to cascading waterfalls, and even land on hidden shores. You become a part of the fjord rather than just an observer.

Personal Reflection: At one point during my paddle in Geirangerfjord, I heard a rustling in the trees along the shore. I paused and watched as a deer emerged, its head tilted inquisitively toward the water. Moments like these—the ones where you truly connect with nature—are why kayaking feels so magical.

2. The Serenity is Unmatched

There's something profoundly meditative about the rhythmic motion of paddling. Without the hum of an engine, you're left alone with the sound of water lapping against your kayak and the distant murmur of wind and wildlife.

What I Observed: In Lysefjord, I experienced moments so quiet that I could hear my own heartbeat. The fjord seemed to breathe around me, its stillness calming my restless thoughts.

3. It's Accessible Yet Adventurous

Fjord kayaking caters to everyone, from first-timers to seasoned paddlers. Local guides provide instruction, making it a safe and enjoyable experience for all.

4. You'll Witness Ever-Changing Scenery

The fjords are dynamic places. Clouds drift through the cliffs, sunlight dances on the water, and every bend reveals a new vista. Each moment feels like discovering a secret only the fjord can tell.

Tips for a Memorable Kayaking Adventure
- Dress in Layers: Even on sunny days, fjord waters can be chilly. Wear moisture-wicking clothing under a windproof jacket.
- Bring Waterproof Gear: Dry bags (€15–€30) are a lifesaver for protecting phones, cameras, and snacks.
- Listen to Your Guide: Local guides are not only skilled paddlers but also storytellers who can share the fjord's history and legends.
- Book in Advance: Tours can fill up quickly, especially during the summer months (June–August).

Practical Information
- When to Go: Late spring to early autumn (May–September) offers the best weather for kayaking.
- Costs: Prices vary depending on the location and tour duration, typically ranging from €50 to €150.
- What to Pack: Sunscreen, reusable water bottles, snacks, and a camera (secured in a dry bag).

Unique wildlife encounters: Puffins, whales, and more

Imagine this: you're perched on a cliff, watching a flock of puffins with their striking beaks dart through the air before diving headlong into the water. Or perhaps you're standing on the deck of a boat, the salty sea breeze in your hair, when a humpback whale breaches nearby, its massive tail carving an elegant arc in the air. These moments, fleeting yet deeply profound, remind you of how alive the world is, how interconnected we are with its creatures.

In Norway, nature doesn't just surround you—it engages you in a conversation. Its wildlife, from playful puffins to majestic whales, takes center stage in a country that feels like a sanctuary for the wild. I've had the privilege of experiencing these encounters firsthand, and they are as magical as they sound. Let me walk you through the best places to witness these awe-inspiring creatures, share my own experiences, and give you all the details you'll need to create your own unforgettable memories.

The Whales of Norway: Giants of the Deep
If you've ever dreamed of seeing whales in their natural habitat, Norway offers some of the most extraordinary opportunities in the world. These majestic creatures grace Norwegian waters during their migrations, and seeing one is nothing short of life-changing.

Where to Go
Tromsø (Northern Norway):
During the winter months (November to January), the waters near Tromsø come alive with humpback whales and orcas, drawn by the bountiful herring.

What to Do: Book a whale-watching safari. Most tours last 3–6 hours and depart from Tromsø's harbor.
Price Range: €150–€200 per person for guided tours.

Vesterålen Archipelago:
For year-round whale watching, the waters around Andenes in Vesterålen are ideal. Sperm whales frequent these depths, diving to hunt squid in one of the world's deepest underwater canyons.
What to Do: Join a guided tour from Andenes. Tours last 4–5 hours, and experienced guides share fascinating insights about these magnificent creatures.
Price Range: €100–€170 per person.

What I Observed
One icy November morning, I boarded a boat in Tromsø, bundled up in layers, the Arctic air sharp against my face. As we ventured into the fjord, the water began to ripple. Suddenly, an orca emerged—a sleek, powerful silhouette against the wintry backdrop. Moments later, a humpback whale breached nearby, its colossal form breaking the surface in a graceful arc. The splash was thunderous, soaking us with icy spray, but I didn't care. I was overcome with awe, tears pricking my eyes at the sheer magnificence of it all.

Puffins: Clowns of the Sea
Puffins may be small, but they have an outsized charm. With their colorful beaks and endearing waddle, these seabirds are a delight to watch. Their skillful dives and bursts of flight are nothing short of mesmerizing.

Where to Go
Runde Island (Sunnmøre Coast):
Known as "Bird Island," Runde is home to over 500,000 seabirds, including a significant puffin colony. The best time to visit is between April and August, during the breeding season.
What to Do: Hike to Runde's cliffs, where puffins nest, or take a guided boat tour around the island for a closer look.
Price Range: Boat tours cost €40–€70.

Hornøya Island (Far Northeast):
For an even more remote experience, visit Hornøya, Norway's easternmost point. The island hosts large puffin colonies as well as razorbills and kittiwakes.
What to Do: Catch a short ferry from Vardø and explore the island on foot.
Price Range: €20–€50 for ferry and entry fees.

What I Observed

On a misty summer morning at Runde, I perched on a grassy cliff overlooking the sea. Puffins flitted back and forth, carrying fish in their beaks to their hidden nests. Their playful nature was infectious. One puffin landed awkwardly nearby, its tiny feet scrambling to balance on a rock. I couldn't help but laugh—it was like watching nature's comedians in action. As they dove into the water with surprising grace, I was struck by how effortlessly they bridged two worlds, air and sea.

Reindeer: Guardians of the Arctic

Reindeer, iconic symbols of the Arctic, roam freely across Norway's northern landscapes. They've been integral to Sami culture for centuries, representing both sustenance and spiritual connection.

Where to Go
Finnmark Region:
The tundra of Finnmark, in Northern Norway, is home to vast herds of reindeer. Guided experiences often include insights into Sami reindeer herding traditions.
What to Do: Book a Sami-led reindeer sledding tour. These excursions typically include a fireside storytelling session inside a traditional lavvu (tent).
Price Range: €100–€200 per person.

What I Observed
In the stillness of the Arctic winter, I found myself sitting in a wooden sled, wrapped in reindeer skins as a team of reindeer pulled me through the snow. Their rhythmic footsteps crunched softly against the frozen ground. Later, around a crackling fire, a Sami elder spoke of the deep bond between his people and the reindeer. As I gazed at the herd grazing nearby, framed by the glow of the Northern Lights, I felt a profound respect for this ancient connection.

Eagles and Seals: Masters of the Fjords

Norway's fjords are alive with wildlife, from soaring eagles to playful seals. These encounters bring a sense of vitality to the serene landscapes.

Where to Go
Trollfjord (Lofoten Islands):
The narrow Trollfjord is an eagle-watching hotspot, where white-tailed eagles glide majestically overhead.
What to Do: Join a RIB (rigid inflatable boat) tour to explore the fjord and get close to the wildlife. (€80–€120).
Personal Tip: Bring binoculars to watch the eagles dive dramatically to catch fish.

Sognefjord:
Seals can often be spotted basking on rocks along Norway's longest fjord. Take a guided kayaking tour (€70–€100) for a closer look.

What I Observed
In Trollfjord, I craned my neck as a white-tailed eagle soared above us, its wings spanning an impressive two meters. It dove suddenly, claws extending, and emerged from the water clutching a fish. The precision and power of the moment left me speechless, the fjord echoing with its triumphant cry.

Why You Should Embark on These Wildlife Adventures

these wildlife encounters are more than just moments of awe—they are reminders of the fragile, interconnected world we share. They teach us to observe, to respect, and to cherish. Here's why you should embark on your own Norwegian wildlife adventure:

- For the Connection: Standing face-to-face with a puffin or watching a whale breach is humbling. It reminds you of the world's vastness and your place within it.
- For the Memories: These experiences stay with you, offering stories and moments to revisit for a lifetime.
- For the Conservation Impact: Many tours contribute to wildlife preservation efforts, making your trip meaningful in ways beyond personal enjoyment.

Experiencing farm visits and local life in fjord-side villages

When I embarked on a journey to explore the farms and villages along Norway's fjords, I didn't just see a landscape—I met a way of life. I discovered stories in every stone, every field, every smile. And I want you to have that same joy. Let me tell you why these experiences are so meaningful, how incredible they were when I tried them, and where to go so you can create your own unforgettable memories.

The Joy of Farm Visits
1. The Fruit Orchards of Hardangerfjord: Sweetness by the Water
Location: Hardangerfjord, often called the "Orchard of Norway," is renowned for its abundant fruit farms.
What to Do:
Visit family-run fruit farms that grow apples, cherries, pears, and plums. During the blooming season in spring (April-May), the orchards transform into seas of white and pink blossoms. In autumn, they become a paradise of ripe, sun-kissed fruit.
Experience:
- Cider Tasting: Many farms, like Aga Sideri and Hardanger Saftog Siderfabrikk, offer cider tastings that let you sip on the flavors of the fjord (€30–€50 for guided tastings).
- Farm Tours: Learn about traditional fruit growing and cider-making techniques passed down for generations.

What I Observed: Wandering through the blooming orchards in Hardangerfjord felt like walking in a dream. The air was filled with the delicate scent of blossoms, and bees buzzed busily among the trees. At one farm, the farmer handed me a freshly picked apple, and with one bite, I tasted the crisp sweetness that could only come from fruit grown in this pure, fjord-side environment.

2. Geiranger's Mountain Farms: Living Above the Fjord

Location: High above Geirangerfjord, these remote farms offer stunning views and a deep dive into Norway's farming history.

What to Do:
- Visit Skageflå Farm: Accessible by hiking or ferry, this abandoned farm perched on a cliff tells a story of resilience and hard work. Once famous for its goat cheese, it is a hauntingly beautiful reminder of life lived on the edge.
- Guided Farm Tours: Some farms, like Herdalssetra, welcome visitors to meet goats and cows, taste homemade cheese, and learn about traditional dairy farming (€10–€20 per person).

What I Observed: The climb to Skageflå was exhilarating, but the view was even more so. Looking down at Geirangerfjord, the fields and terraces seemed impossibly small against the vast landscape. I couldn't help but imagine the families who lived here, tending their goats while surrounded by such overpowering beauty. Their courage and ingenuity left me in awe.

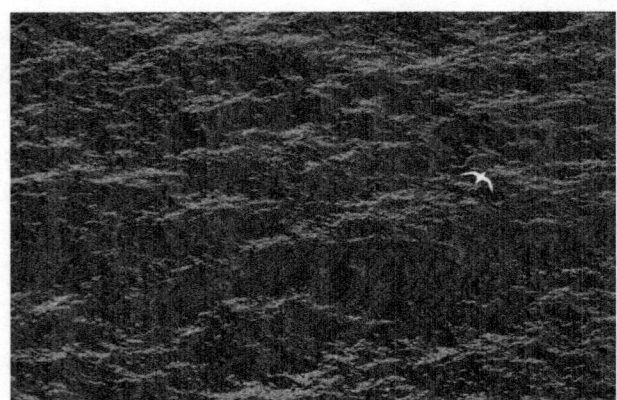

3. A Taste of Sami Culture in Finnmark

Location: Northern Norway's Finnmark region is home to the Sami people, whose reindeer-herding traditions offer a unique glimpse into Arctic farm life.

What to Do:
- Reindeer Sledding: Take part in this traditional Sami activity, followed by feeding and herding demonstrations (€100–€200 per person).
- Lavvu Dinners: Share a meal inside a Sami tent, complete with storytelling and joik (traditional Sami singing).

What I Observed: Watching the Sami herders interact with their reindeer was mesmerizing. Each animal seemed to recognize its name, trotting obediently yet spiritedly after its owner. Later, as I sat in a lavvu beside a glowing fire, the warmth of the Sami hospitality matched only the rich flavors of the reindeer stew they shared with me.

Exploring Fjord-Side Villages

1. Undredal: The Little Village of Goats and Cheese

Location: Nestled along Aurlandsfjord, near Flåm.

Why Visit: Home to more goats than people, Undredal is famous for its goat cheese (geitost) and picturesque charm.

What to Do:
- Cheese Tastings: Visit a local dairy to sample creamy goat cheese, including the famous brown cheese with its sweet, caramel-like flavor (€10–€20).

~ 78 ~

- Stave Church Tour: Explore Norway's smallest stave church, built in 1147.

What I Observed: Walking through Undredal felt like stepping into a postcard. I was greeted by the gentle bleats of goats grazing along the fjord. At a local café, I tried goat cheese on freshly baked bread—a taste so rich and unique that it lingered long after I left.

2. Reine: A Crown Jewel of the Lofoten Islands

Location: Lofoten Islands, Northern Norway.

Why Visit: Known for its red fishing cabins (rorbuer) and dramatic peaks, Reine is a perfect blend of natural beauty and cultural heritage.

What to Do:
- Rorbuer Stay: Spend a night in a traditional fishing cabin (€150–€300 per night).
- Fishing Expeditions: Join local fishermen for a taste of Norway's cod fishing tradition (€100–€150).
- What I Observed: Staying in a rorbuer was an experience like no other. The sound of the waves lulled me to sleep, and in the morning, I joined a local fisherman for a trip into the fjord. As we pulled up a net teeming with cod, his laughter rang out, carrying the joy of a life lived close to nature.

3. Flåm: A Hub of Heritage and Scenic Bliss

Location: At the innermost point of Aurlandsfjord.

Why Visit: Flåm is a gateway to some of Norway's most iconic fjord experiences, including the Flåm Railway and scenic boat tours.

What to Do:
- Farm Visits: Stop by Otternes Bygdetun, a cluster of historic farmhouses offering insights into rural Norwegian life (€10–€15).
- Local Markets: Browse stalls selling handmade crafts, jams, and cheeses.

What I Observed: At Otternes Bygdetun, I watched a woman spinning wool by hand, the rhythmic motion so hypnotic I forgot the world around me. She spoke of her grandmother, who had done the same on this very farm—keeping tradition alive, thread by thread.

Why You Should Experience Farm Visits and Fjord-Side Life

farm visits and village explorations aren't just about seeing a place—they're about feeling it. They're about connecting with people whose lives are intertwined with the land, tasting the fruits of their labor, and hearing the stories that make these places come alive.

- For the Connection: These experiences are deeply personal. You'll leave not just with memories but with a sense of belonging, as though you've touched the heart of Norway.
- For the Stories: Every farm, every village has its tales—of resilience, creativity, and harmony with nature.
- For the Flavors: Whether it's goat cheese in Undredal or cider in Hardangerfjord, the taste of these places lingers long after you've left.

When I walked these trails, tasted these foods, and met these people, I felt a part of something timeless. I want you to feel that too. So pack your curiosity, your appetite, and your love of adventure—and let the fjords welcome you into their embrace.

Chapter 8: Culinary Adventures

Traditional Norwegian flavors: From fresh seafood to reindeer

When I explored Norway, tasting my way through its unique culinary traditions was a revelation. I experienced flavors that spoke of simplicity and freshness, yet left a profound impression. Let me take you on this gastronomic journey, from the fishing villages on the coast to the Sami heartlands of the Arctic. Trust me, these are not just dishes—they are memories waiting to be savored.

The Crown Jewel: Fresh Seafood

The cold, pristine waters surrounding Norway are a source of life, yielding some of the finest seafood in the world. The flavors are as pure as the waters they come from, and every bite carries the freshness of the sea.

1. Salmon (Laks)
Why It's Special: Norwegian salmon is internationally renowned for its quality. Whether smoked, grilled, or served raw as

sashimi, its buttery texture and rich flavor are unparalleled.
Signature Dish: Gravlaks (cured salmon) is a classic preparation, where the fish is cured with salt, sugar, and dill, resulting in a delicately sweet and savory flavor.
My Experience: I sat by a fjord in Bergen, savoring a plate of gravlaks served with mustard sauce and freshly baked rye bread. The combination of flavors—the softness of the fish, the tanginess of the mustard, the earthiness of the bread—was unforgettable. It was as though the fjord itself had been plated for me to taste.

2. Arctic Char (Røye)
Why It's Special: Found in the icy waters of the Arctic, Arctic char is similar to salmon but with a more delicate, slightly nutty flavor.
Signature Dish: Pan-seared Arctic char served with root vegetables and a light butter sauce.
What I Observed: In Tromsø, I watched a chef expertly sear Arctic char, the skin crisping to golden perfection. The first bite melted in my mouth, the freshness so evident it felt as though the fish had leapt from the water moments before.

3. Cod (Torsk)
Why It's Special: Norwegian cod, especially skrei (winter cod), is a staple of the country's fishing heritage. Its mild flavor and flaky texture make it incredibly versatile.
Signature Dish: Bacalao, a hearty stew of dried and salted cod, potatoes, tomatoes, and olives, reflects both Norwegian and Spanish influences.
What I Observed: In Ålesund, I tried a steaming bowl of bacalao while listening to fishermen share tales of their trade. Each spoonful carried the warmth and richness of a dish that has sustained generations.

4. King Crab (Kongekrabbe)
Why It's Special: Harvested from Norway's Arctic waters, king crab is a luxury delicacy prized for its sweet, tender meat.
Where to Try It: Take a king crab safari in Kirkenes (€200–€300), where you'll catch your own crab before enjoying a feast.
My Experience: Cracking open a king crab leg on a snowy evening in Kirkenes, I felt an immediate sense of satisfaction. The meat was so sweet and succulent, it needed no embellishment—a true gift from the sea.

Meat and Game: The Flavors of the Land
Norway's vast wilderness is home to unique game meats that reflect the country's deep connection to its environment. These dishes tell stories of the hunt, of survival, and of living in harmony with nature.

1. Reindeer (Reinsdyr)
Why It's Special: Reindeer meat is lean, tender, and slightly sweet, with a flavor reminiscent of venison but milder. It's a central part of Sami cuisine, often cooked simply to highlight its natural taste.
Signature Dish: Bidos, a traditional Sami stew made with reindeer, potatoes, carrots, and onions. Served hot, it's the epitome of comfort food.

My Experience: In a Sami lavvu (tent) near Finnmark, I shared a bowl of bidos by a roaring fire. The reindeer meat was so tender it practically dissolved, and the hearty broth was like a hug in a bowl. The Sami elder who served it to me spoke of reindeer as both sustenance and spiritual companion, adding an emotional depth to every bite.

2. Moose (Elg)
Why It's Special: Moose is the largest land animal in Norway, and its meat is rich and robust, often served as steaks or in hearty stews.
Where to Try It: Many rural restaurants, especially in the forests of Eastern Norway, feature moose dishes on their menus.
What I Observed: The moose steak I tried in a cozy cabin near Lillehammer was served with lingonberry sauce and roasted potatoes. The tangy sweetness of the berries perfectly balanced the meat's deep, earthy flavor.

3. Lamb (Lammekjøtt)
Why It's Special: Norwegian lambs graze on wild herbs and grasses, giving the meat a unique, herbaceous flavor.
Signature Dish: Fårikål, Norway's national dish, is a simple yet delicious stew of lamb, cabbage, and peppercorns, slow-cooked until the meat falls off the bone.
What I Observed: In Hardangerfjord, I sat at a family farm table as a pot of fårikål was placed before us. The aromas of lamb and cabbage filled the room, and with the first spoonful, I understood why this dish is so beloved—it was rustic, honest, and utterly satisfying.

The Sweet Side: Norwegian Desserts

No culinary journey is complete without indulging your sweet tooth, and Norway offers delights as pure and comforting as its landscapes.

1. Krumkake
What It Is: Thin, crisp waffle cookies rolled into cone shapes, often filled with whipped cream or berries.
What I Observed: In Bergen, I watched an elderly woman expertly roll krumkake while sharing stories of how her grandmother taught her the recipe. Each bite was a perfect balance of delicate crispness and sweet creaminess.

2. Cloudberries (Multekrem)
What It Is: A dessert of whipped cream mixed with cloudberries, a rare Arctic berry with a tart yet honeyed flavor.
What I Observed: In Tromsø, I tasted multekrem during the Polar Night. The golden berries seemed to glow against the whipped cream, and their flavor was as rare and special as the moment itself.

Why You Should Embrace Norwegian Flavors
experiencing Norwegian cuisine is like tasting the country's essence. It's a chance to connect with the fjords, the forests, and the Arctic tundra through the flavors they produce. Here's why you should dive in:

- For the Purity: Norwegian ingredients are as pristine as the landscapes they come from, offering flavors that are fresh, clean, and deeply satisfying.
- For the Stories: Every dish has a tale—of fishermen braving Arctic waters, of Sami traditions passed

through generations, of farmers nurturing their land.
- For the Connection: Sharing a meal in Norway is more than sustenance—it's an invitation to become part of its culture and history.

Best local dishes to try at each port

Bergen: The Seafood Capital
Bergen's proximity to the North Sea makes it a haven for seafood lovers. The city's vibrant fish market, Fisketorget, is the heart of its culinary scene.

Must-Try Dishes
1. Gravlaks (Cured Salmon)
What It Is: Thinly sliced salmon cured with a mix of sugar, salt, and dill. Often served with mustard sauce and rye bread.
What I Experienced: Sitting at an outdoor table by the fish market, I savored gravlaks while the salty sea breeze filled the air. The balance of sweet, salty, and herbal flavors felt like the essence of Bergen captured on a plate.

2. Bergen Fish Soup (Bergensk Fiskesuppe)
What It Is: A creamy soup made with fish stock, cream, vegetables, and delicate chunks of fish or shellfish.
Where to Try: Cornelius Seafood Restaurant (€25–€40).

What I Observed: The soup's richness, paired with the briny taste of fresh seafood, was like wrapping yourself in a warm blanket on a rainy Bergen day.

Ålesund: Art Nouveau and Traditional Flavors
Nestled amid stunning fjords, Ålesund is a gem for both architecture lovers and foodies. Its location ensures access to the freshest seafood.

Must-Try Dishes
1. Bacalao
What It Is: A hearty stew made with dried and salted cod, potatoes, tomatoes, and olives. Reflects Ålesund's fishing heritage and its ties to Southern Europe.
What I Observed: The tanginess of the tomatoes and the saltiness of the cod created a perfect harmony. As I sipped the stew in a cozy restaurant, I felt transported through the city's history as a global fishing hub.

2. Klippfisk (Salted Cod)
What It Is: Codfish preserved through salting and drying, prepared in a variety of ways—grilled, baked, or fried. Often served with potatoes and vegetables.
Where to Try: XL Diner (€30–€50), known for its creative takes on klippfisk.

Stavanger: Culinary Art Meets Comfort

Known for its mix of history and modernity, Stavanger offers hearty dishes that reflect its agricultural roots and coastal location.

Must-Try Dishes

1. Lobscouse (Lapskaus)
What It Is: A traditional Norwegian stew made with beef or lamb, potatoes, carrots, and onions, slow-cooked to perfection.
What I Experienced: Lapskaus in Stavanger tasted like home—a dish so warm and hearty, it could ward off even the chilliest of Norwegian winds. Each spoonful brought comfort, paired with crusty bread fresh from the oven.

2. Brunost (Brown Cheese)
What It Is: A caramelized cheese with a sweet yet tangy flavor, typically served on waffles or bread.
What I Observed: At a local café, I spread brunost on freshly baked bread. Its unique taste—a mix of sweet and savory—was unlike anything I'd ever tried. It's a must for anyone visiting Stavanger.

Tromsø: Arctic Delicacies

Tromsø's location above the Arctic Circle means its cuisine is shaped by the extreme north—think reindeer, Arctic char, and king crab.

Must-Try Dishes

1. King Crab
What It Is: Sweet, tender crab meat harvested from the icy Arctic waters. Often steamed and served with melted butter or a squeeze of lemon.
Where to Try: On a king crab safari in Kirkenes or local Tromsø restaurants (€100–€200).
What I Experienced: Cracking open a king crab leg, the meat inside was so fresh and sweet it felt like a true Arctic indulgence.

2. Reindeer Stew (Bidos)
What It Is: A Sami specialty made with tender chunks of reindeer, potatoes, and carrots in a light broth.
What I Observed: Sharing a bowl of bidos in a Sami lavvu, with the Northern Lights shimmering above, was one of the most memorable meals of my life. It wasn't just food—it was a connection to Arctic culture.

Flåm: Rustic Simplicity

Flåm's charm lies in its small village atmosphere and focus on wholesome, locally sourced ingredients.

Must-Try Dishes

1. Geitost (Goat Cheese)

What It Is: A sweet and caramel-like cheese made from goat's milk.

Where to Try: Local dairies in nearby Undredal (€10–€20 for tastings).

What I Observed: Tasting geitost at a farm in Undredal, surrounded by grazing goats and the Aurlandsfjord, was an unforgettable experience. The cheese's richness reflected the lushness of its surroundings.

2. Kjøttkaker (Meatballs)

What It Is: Norwegian meatballs served with mashed potatoes, gravy, and lingonberry jam.

What I Experienced: At a small eatery in Flåm, I found myself savoring kjøttkaker alongside a glass of local cider. The combination of sweet lingonberries and savory meat was simple yet divine.

Geiranger: A Taste of the High Cliffs

Geirangerfjord's dramatic scenery is matched by its rustic, hearty cuisine that draws from the surrounding mountains and waters.

Must-Try Dishes

1. Rakfisk (Fermented Fish)

What It Is: Trout that's salted and fermented for months, then served with potatoes, flatbread, and sour cream.

What I Observed: Rakfisk is not for the faint-hearted, but its bold, tangy flavor is unlike anything else. Tasting it on a farm above Geirangerfjord, with the scent of fresh mountain air and the view of the fjord below, made it a daring yet rewarding experience.

2. Norwegian Waffles

What It Is: Heart-shaped waffles served with sour cream, jam, or brunost.

What I Experienced: Warm waffles at a hillside café after a morning hike—it was the perfect blend of comfort and sweetness, the ideal reward for exploring the fjord.

Why You Should Explore Norway Through Its Flavors

tasting the local dishes at each fjord port isn't just about the food—it's about the connection. It's about sitting down with a plate of something crafted with care and tradition, and in that moment, becoming part of the story of the land and its people. Each bite is an introduction, a memory, a love letter from Norway to your senses.

Café culture and must-visit restaurants

Café culture in Norway is deeply intertwined with the concept of koselig (similar to the

Danish hygge), which emphasizes coziness, warmth, and enjoying life's little pleasures. Here are some highlights of what makes it special:

- A Focus on Coffee: Norwegians are among the world's most avid coffee drinkers, and their love for it is reflected in their thriving café scene. Whether it's a simple black coffee (sort kaffe) or a frothy cappuccino, quality is paramount.
- A Slower Pace: Norwegian cafés invite you to linger. There's no rush to leave your table; in fact, it's encouraged to take your time and enjoy the moment.
- The Local Touch: Many cafés prioritize local ingredients, from milk and butter in their pastries to berries and jams used as toppings.

Must-Visit Cafés Across Norway

1. Tim Wendelboe (Oslo)
What It's Known For: Named after one of the world's leading coffee experts, this café and roastery in Oslo is a mecca for coffee enthusiasts.
What to Try: A single-origin pour-over, brewed to perfection.
What I Observed: The minimalist interior lets the coffee take center stage. I watched baristas expertly measure, pour, and present each cup like a work of art. The result? A coffee so smooth and balanced, it felt like tasting the essence of the bean itself.

2. Kaffemisjonen (Bergen)
What It's Known For: Bergen's best-kept secret for specialty coffee, with an inviting atmosphere perfect for rainy afternoons.
What to Try: A classic flat white paired with a slice of carrot cake.
What I Observed: The sound of gentle jazz, the aroma of freshly brewed coffee, and the warmth of a wooden table made this café feel like a haven from the outside world.

3. Buvette (Stavanger)
What It's Known For: A charming café serving artisanal coffee and simple, locally inspired dishes.
What to Try: Their freshly baked cinnamon buns and a latte made with locally sourced milk.
What I Observed: The café's bright interior, dotted with greenery, created a serene and welcoming vibe. I found myself lingering longer than planned, savoring every bite and sip.

4. Risø (Tromsø)

What It's Known For: A cozy café in the heart of Tromsø, blending Northern charm with top-quality brews.
What to Try: A rich hot chocolate made with Norwegian chocolate—perfect for Arctic winters.
What I Observed: Gazing out the window at snow-dusted streets while cradling a mug of hot chocolate was like experiencing pure Arctic magic.

Norway's Must-Visit Restaurants: A Gastronomic Journey

From coastal seafood to reindeer dishes steeped in Sami tradition, Norway's restaurant scene reflects the country's incredible diversity. Here are some must-visit spots for a true taste of Norway.

1. Maaemo (Oslo)
What It's Known For: As Norway's first three-Michelin-star restaurant, Maaemo offers a sensory dining experience that highlights the purity of Norwegian ingredients.
What to Try: The seasonal tasting menu, which often includes reindeer, scallops, and cloudberries. (€300–€400 per person).
What I Observed: Every dish was like a painting—a delicate balance of colors and textures. The flavors were bold yet refined, a celebration of Norway's natural bounty.

2. Lysverket (Bergen)
What It's Known For: Modern seafood dishes with a Norwegian twist, located in Bergen's historic art museum.
What to Try: The shellfish platter, featuring langoustines and Arctic char. (€80–€120 per person).
What I Observed: The restaurant's sleek, minimalist design was the perfect backdrop for the vibrant dishes. Each bite of seafood tasted like the ocean itself, fresh and full of life.

3. Sabi Omakase (Stavanger)
What It's Known For: Michelin-starred sushi crafted with Nordic ingredients and Japanese precision.
What to Try: The omakase menu, featuring delicacies like Arctic cod and sea urchin. (€200–€300 per person).
What I Observed: Watching the chef prepare each piece of sushi was mesmerizing. The care and respect for each ingredient were evident in every bite.

4. Smak (Tromsø)
What It's Known For: A fine dining experience in the Arctic, focusing on local and seasonal ingredients.
What to Try: A tasting menu that might include reindeer, Arctic char, and foraged mushrooms. (€150–€250 per person).
What I Observed: The dishes felt like a journey through the Arctic, with flavors that were earthy, fresh, and deeply rooted in the region's identity.

Why You Should Dive Into Norway's Café Culture and Restaurants

exploring Norway's cafés and restaurants is not just about satisfying your hunger—it's about experiencing the heart of the country. Every cup of coffee, every bite of food, is an invitation to connect with Norway's traditions, landscapes, and people.

- For the Warmth: In Norway's cafés, you'll find a cozy escape from the cold, where a simple coffee becomes a moment of pure joy.
- For the Flavors: Whether it's freshly caught cod, reindeer stew, or a slice of krumkake, the dishes reflect the beauty and bounty of the land.
- For the Stories: Behind every plate is a story—of a farmer tending their fields, a chef creating art, or a fisherman braving the fjords.

When I look back on my time in Norway, it's these moments—cradling a warm cup of coffee in Bergen, savoring Arctic char in Tromsø—that stand out. They were more than meals—they were memories, rich with flavor and meaning.

Crafting the perfect onboard dining experience

1. Setting the Mood: The Importance of Ambiance

The setting of your onboard dining experience is as essential as the meal itself. The fjords provide a natural backdrop of unparalleled beauty, so it's important to create an atmosphere that complements the landscape.

Dining with a View

Where to Sit: Opt for a table by the window or, weather permitting, dine on the outdoor deck for uninterrupted views of the fjords. The towering cliffs, still waters, and ever-changing skies are the ultimate dining companions.

What I Observed: On one serene evening, as the boat glided through Nærøyfjord, I dined on a table by the window. The fading sunlight painted the cliffs in hues of gold and amber, casting their reflection on the water. The view itself was as much a part of the meal as the food on my plate.

Lighting and Music

Soft, warm lighting sets a cozy tone for evening meals, while natural light spilling into the dining room during the day creates a fresh, inviting atmosphere. Pair this with gentle acoustic or classical music to enhance the feeling of relaxation and intimacy.

2. Savoring Norway's Culinary Identity

Norwegian cuisine is rooted in tradition, simplicity, and a profound connection to the land and sea. A perfect onboard dining experience embraces these elements, offering dishes that reflect the essence of the fjords.

Signature Dishes to Include
1. Fresh Seafood
- Salmon and Arctic Char: Whether grilled, smoked, or cured as gravlaks, these fish are staples of Norwegian dining. Their flavor is fresh, light, and perfectly representative of the fjords.
- King Crab: A delicacy from the Arctic waters, its sweet, tender meat is a highlight of any meal.

What I Experienced: I still remember the first bite of smoked salmon served on rye bread, topped with dill and a hint of lemon. The flavors were as crisp and refreshing as the mountain air outside.

2. Lamb and Reindeer
Sourced from Norwegian farms and tundra, these meats are often served in stews or grilled to perfection. Reindeer dishes carry a slightly sweet, earthy flavor that's both unique and memorable.

3. Fjord Trout
Fjord trout is prized for its delicate flavor and tender texture. Served as a main course or as an appetizer in tartare form, it never fails to impress.

4. Traditional Soups and Stews
- Bergen Fish Soup: Creamy and comforting, this soup is a must-try dish on fjord cruises.
- Fårikål: Norway's national dish, a hearty lamb and cabbage stew, provides warmth and comfort on cooler days.

Sweet Finishes
- Norwegian Waffles: Heart-shaped waffles served with brunost (brown cheese) and berry jam are a delightful treat to end your meal.
- Multekrem: A dessert made with cloudberries folded into whipped cream, its flavor is as special as the rare Arctic berries themselves.

3. Pairing Food with Norway's Local Beverages

No onboard dining experience is complete without the perfect drink to accompany your meal. Norway's beverages, whether traditional or contemporary, enhance the flavors of its cuisine.

Drinks to Consider
Cider from Hardangerfjord: Locally produced ciders, often crafted from apples grown in fjord-side orchards, are crisp and refreshing—a perfect match for seafood dishes.

What I Observed: Sipping a glass of Hardanger cider as I dined on grilled trout felt like tasting the orchard and the fjord in one harmonious moment.

- Akvavit: Norway's signature spirit, distilled with caraway and herbs, pairs wonderfully with salmon or cured meats.
- Local Beer: Fjord-side breweries produce craft beers that complement both hearty stews and light fish dishes.
- Lingonberry Juice: For non-alcoholic options, this tart, fruity drink is a refreshing accompaniment to any meal.

4. Creating Unforgettable Dining Moments
A great meal is more than just food—it's the moments shared, the stories told, and the special touches that make it memorable. Here's how to make your onboard dining experience truly extraordinary:

Chef Demonstrations
Many fjord cruises offer cooking demonstrations, allowing you to watch chefs prepare traditional Norwegian dishes. It's a fascinating way to learn about local ingredients and techniques while adding a

touch of entertainment to your dining experience.

Themed Dinners
- Seafood Feast: Dedicate one evening to the bounty of the fjords, featuring lobster, crab, prawns, and fish prepared in various styles.
- Viking-Inspired Dinner: Serve hearty dishes like lamb stews and flatbreads, paired with mead or ale, to transport diners to Norway's Viking past.

Celebrating the Seasons
- Summer Evenings: Dine alfresco under the midnight sun, with light, refreshing dishes like salads and grilled fish.
- Winter Nights: Embrace the coziness of Polar Night with warm, hearty meals served in candlelit dining rooms.

5. Why Onboard Dining is a Must-Do
onboard dining isn't just about convenience—it's about connection. It's about savoring flavors that reflect the landscapes you're sailing through, about taking a moment to slow down and truly appreciate your surroundings.

- For the Views: Dining with the fjords as your backdrop adds an element of wonder to every bite.
- For the Flavors: The food is fresh, local, and deeply tied to Norwegian tradition.
- For the Memories: Shared meals onboard become stories you carry with you, moments of joy and discovery that linger long after your journey ends.

Chapter 9: ACCOMMODATION

Luxury Hotels: Where to experience opulence and panoramic fjord views.

1. Hotel Ullensvang (Hardangerfjord)

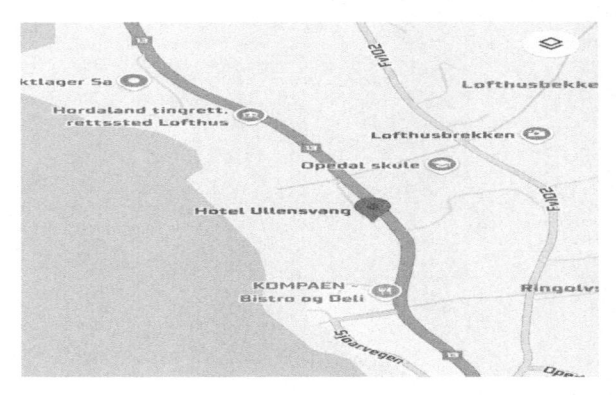

Location
Nestled along the shores of Hardangerfjord, Hotel Ullensvang is a family-run gem that has been welcoming guests for over 170 years. It's located in Lofthus, a charming village surrounded by fruit orchards and snow-capped peaks.

Getting There
- By Car: A scenic 2.5-hour drive from Bergen, following the Hardanger National Tourist Route.
- By Public Transport: Take a train from Bergen to Voss, then a bus to Lofthus.

What to Expect
- Rooms and Suites: Elegantly designed with floor-to-ceiling windows that frame the fjord. Prices range from €250–€500 per night, depending on the season and room type.
- Infinity Pool: Swim in a heated infinity pool that seems to merge with the fjord itself.

- Dining: The hotel's restaurant serves locally inspired dishes, including Hardangerfjord trout and apple desserts made from the region's famous orchards.

What to Do
- Hike to Trolltunga: The hotel is a perfect base for this iconic hike.
- Explore the Orchards: Visit nearby fruit farms and cider houses for tastings.
- Relax in the Spa: Indulge in a massage while gazing at the fjord.

What I Observed
As I lounged by the infinity pool, the fjord stretched out before me like a living painting. The water mirrored the mountains, and the only sound was the gentle lapping of waves. Later, as I dined on freshly caught trout, the setting sun bathed the room in golden light. It was a moment of pure serenity.

2. Kviknes Hotel (Balestrand, Sognefjord)
Location
Perched on the edge of Sognefjord, Kviknes Hotel is a historic property that combines old-world charm with modern luxury. Its location in Balestrand offers panoramic views of the fjord and surrounding mountains.

Getting There
- By Boat: Take an express boat from Bergen to Balestrand (4 hours).
- By Car: A 3.5-hour drive from Bergen, including a ferry crossing.

What to Expect
- Rooms and Suites: Choose between the historic wing, with antique furnishings, or the modern wing, with sleek, contemporary designs. Prices range from €200–€400 per night.
- Art and History: The hotel is adorned with paintings and artifacts that tell the story of its rich heritage.
- Dining: The restaurant offers a seasonal menu featuring local ingredients, such as lamb from nearby farms and berries from the mountains.

What to Do
- Fjord Cruises: Explore Sognefjord by boat, stopping at charming villages along the way.
- Hiking and Biking: Trails around Balestrand offer stunning views and peaceful solitude.
- Visit St. Olaf's Church: A picturesque stave church just a short walk from the hotel.

What I Observed

The view from my balcony was nothing short of magical. The fjord shimmered in the moonlight, and the mountains stood like silent sentinels. As I sipped a glass of local cider, I felt a deep sense of gratitude for the beauty around me.

3. Hotel Union (Geirangerfjord)

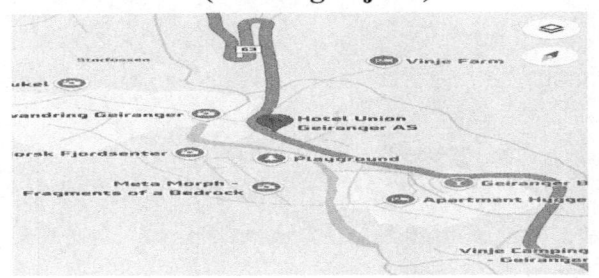

Location
Overlooking the UNESCO-listed Geirangerfjord, Hotel Union is a luxurious retreat that offers unparalleled views of one of Norway's most famous fjords.

Getting There
- By Car: A 6-hour drive from Bergen or a 2.5-hour drive from Ålesund.
- By Public Transport: Take a bus from Ålesund to Geiranger.

What to Expect
- Rooms and Suites: Spacious and elegantly furnished, with balconies that open to fjord views. Prices range from €300–€600 per night.
- Wellness Center: A spa with outdoor hot tubs, saunas, and treatments inspired by Nordic traditions.
- Dining: The restaurant serves gourmet dishes, including reindeer steak and cloudberry desserts.

What to Do
- Fjord Sightseeing: Take a boat tour to see the Seven Sisters and Suitor waterfalls.
- Hike to Skageflå: A historic mountain farm with breathtaking views.
- Relax in the Pool: Swim in the outdoor pool while gazing at the fjord.

What I Observed
From the hotel's terrace, I watched as the morning mist lifted from the fjord, revealing its emerald waters. The sight was so mesmerizing that I found myself lingering long after breakfast, simply soaking in the view.

4. Britannia Hotel (Trondheim)

Location
Located in the heart of Trondheim, Britannia Hotel is a five-star property that combines luxury with a rich history dating back to 1870.

Getting There
- By Plane: Fly into Trondheim Airport, then take a 30-minute taxi or train ride to the city center.
- By Train: Trondheim is well-connected by rail to other major Norwegian cities.

What to Expect
- Rooms and Suites: Lavishly decorated with plush furnishings and modern amenities. Prices range from €400–€800 per night.
- Spa and Wellness: A luxurious spa offering treatments, a pool, and a relaxation area.
- Dining: The hotel's Speilsalen restaurant holds a Michelin star and offers an exquisite tasting menu.

What to Do
- Explore Nidaros Cathedral: A stunning Gothic cathedral just a short walk from the hotel.
- Visit Bakklandet: Trondheim's charming old town, filled with colorful wooden houses and cafés.
- Fjord Excursions: Take a boat tour to explore the Trondheim Fjord.

What I Observed
The Britannia Hotel felt like stepping into a world of elegance. From the grand chandeliers in the lobby to the impeccable service, every detail was designed to make you feel special. The tasting menu at Speilsalen was a culinary journey, with each dish more inventive and delicious than the last.

Mid-Range and Budget Hotels: Comfortable stays for every traveler.

1. Marken Guesthouse (Bergen)
Location
Nestled in the heart of Bergen, Marken Guesthouse is just a stone's throw from the iconic Bryggen Wharf and the bustling Fish Market. Its prime location makes it an ideal choice for exploring this vibrant, historic city.

Getting There
- By Train: From Bergen Station, it's just a 5-minute walk to the guesthouse.
- By Taxi: If arriving by plane, a 20-minute taxi ride from Bergen Airport will take you directly there.

What to Expect
- Rooms and Prices: Offers a mix of private rooms and dormitories. Private rooms range from €80–€120 per night, while dorm beds start at €30–€50, making it an excellent choice for solo travelers and families alike.
- Facilities: Shared kitchens and lounge areas, perfect for cooking your own meals and meeting other travelers.
- Design: Clean, minimalistic decor with splashes of Scandinavian charm.

What to Do Nearby
- Explore Bryggen Wharf: Just a short walk away, this UNESCO World Heritage Site is a must-see.
- Ride the Fløibanen Funicular: Ascend Mount Fløyen for panoramic views of the city and fjord below.
- Indulge in Seafood: The Fish Market is nearby, where you can sample fresh salmon, shrimp, and king crab.

What I Observed
The vibe at Marken Guesthouse was refreshingly lively yet tranquil. The common areas were alive with conversation—travelers sharing stories over cups of coffee. From my dorm window, I could see the rooftops of Bergen and hear the occasional call of seagulls echoing through the alleyways. It was the kind of place where you immediately felt part of a community.

2. Flåm Hostel (Flåm)
Location
Situated in the tiny village of Flåm, surrounded by towering cliffs and the sparkling Aurlandsfjord, Flåm Hostel is a picturesque haven for travelers seeking both comfort and adventure.

Getting There
- By Train: Arrive on the world-famous Flåm Railway, which connects to Myrdal Station on the Bergen Line. The hostel is just a 10-minute walk from the Flåm train station.
- By Car: A scenic 2.5-hour drive from Bergen.

What to Expect
- Rooms and Prices: Offers private rooms (€90–€150 per night) and shared dormitories (€50–€70). The rooms are cozy, clean, and decorated in classic Nordic style.
- Facilities: Fully equipped kitchens and outdoor picnic areas, where you can enjoy your meals with a view of the fjord.
- Ambiance: Quiet and serene, with a strong focus on eco-conscious living.

What to Do Nearby
- Fjord Cruises: Take a boat tour along Nærøyfjord, one of the narrowest fjords in the world.
- Hike the Aurlandsdalen Valley: Known as Norway's Grand Canyon, it's a hiker's paradise.
- Visit Stegastein Viewpoint: A short drive away, this platform juts out over the fjord for jaw-dropping views.

What I Observed
Flåm Hostel was a sanctuary. I spent my evenings sitting on the patio, watching the light play on the fjord as the mountains turned dark in silhouette. The staff were wonderfully kind, sharing tips on hidden hiking trails and local traditions. There was a peaceful energy about the place, as though the fjord itself had slowed time.

3. Thon Hotel Tromsø (Tromsø)
Location
Located in the heart of Tromsø, Thon Hotel Tromsø is perfect for exploring the Arctic capital. It's within walking distance of the city's main attractions, yet tucked away enough to feel quiet and intimate.

Getting There
- By Plane: A 15-minute taxi ride from Tromsø Airport Langnes.
- By Bus: Take the Flybussen (airport bus) to the city center; the hotel is a 5-minute walk from the stop.

What to Expect

- Rooms and Prices: Modern, comfortable rooms with vibrant decor. Prices range from €120–€180 per night, including a delicious breakfast buffet.
- Facilities: Free Wi-Fi, 24-hour reception, and cozy lounge areas.

What to Do Nearby
- Northern Lights Tours: Tromsø is one of the best places in the world to see the aurora borealis during winter.
- Visit Polaria: A unique Arctic aquarium just a short walk from the hotel.
- Arctic Cathedral: Tromsø's iconic triangular church is a 15-minute stroll away.

What I Observed
Thon Hotel Tromsø felt warm and inviting, even in the chill of the Arctic winter. After a day spent chasing the Northern Lights, I returned to a cozy room filled with thoughtful touches, like a plush chair by the window where I could sip tea while gazing out at the snow-dusted streets.

4. Hotel Vangsgaarden (Aurland)
Location
Located in the idyllic village of Aurland, just minutes from the UNESCO-listed Nærøyfjord, Vangsgaarden is a charming waterfront hotel with a rich history.

Getting There
- By Car: A 2.5-hour drive from Bergen via the E16.
- By Bus: Take a bus from Flåm or Voss; the hotel is a short walk from the bus stop.

What to Expect
- Rooms and Prices: Traditional rooms in a historic building (€100–€160) or cozy waterfront cabins (€150–€200).
- Facilities: On-site restaurant serving local dishes, and a garden overlooking the fjord.
- Ambiance: Rustic yet refined, with an emphasis on hospitality.

What to Do Nearby
- Explore the Aurlandsfjord: Rent a kayak or take a guided tour.
- Hike to Prest Viewpoint: A moderately challenging hike with rewarding views of the fjord.
- Visit Undredal: A nearby village famous for its goat cheese.

What I Observed
From my cabin's porch, I watched boats glide across the fjord in the early morning light. The air was crisp, carrying the scent of saltwater and pine. It felt like stepping into another world, where life moved at a gentler pace.

Cabins and Cottages: Cozy retreats close to nature.

1. Flam Cabins (Flåm)
Location
Flåm Cabins are located in the picturesque village of Flåm, surrounded by the towering cliffs and sparkling waters of the Aurlandsfjord. A perfect base for fjord explorers.

Getting There
- By Train: Flåm is the terminus of the Flåm Railway, one of the most scenic train rides in the world. It connects to the Bergen Line at Myrdal Station.
- By Car: A 2.5-hour drive from Bergen along the E16.
- By Boat: Flåm is a port of call for fjord cruises, making it accessible via water.

What to Expect
- Prices: €100–€200 per night, depending on the season and cabin size.
- Features: These charming wooden cabins are rustic yet modern, equipped with kitchens, cozy beds, and private patios that overlook the fjord. Some even have small gardens.
- Ambiance: Quiet, with the soothing sound of the river flowing nearby.

What to Do Nearby
- Fjord Safari: Take a high-speed RIB boat tour to explore the Nærøyfjord and Aurlandsfjord.
- Flåm Railway: Ride this famous train for dramatic views of waterfalls, mountains, and valleys.
- Hike to Brekkefossen: A short but steep trail that rewards you with panoramic views of Flåm and the fjord below.

What I Observed
Waking up in Flåm Cabins felt like stepping into a fairytale. The morning mist clung to the cliffs, and the fjord shimmered in the soft light of dawn. As I sipped my coffee on the patio, a pair of swans glided gracefully across the water. The world felt impossibly still, as though nature itself had paused to let me savor the moment.

2. Geirangerfjorden Feriesenter (Geiranger)

Location
Tucked along the shores of Geirangerfjord, one of Norway's most iconic fjords, these cottages offer front-row seats to nature's drama.

Getting There
- By Car: A 6-hour drive from Bergen or a 2.5-hour drive from Ålesund, following the scenic Golden Route.
- By Ferry: Geiranger is accessible by ferry from Hellesylt, offering spectacular views along the way.

What to Expect
- Prices: €120–€250 per night, depending on the cottage size and amenities.
- Features: Spacious and well-furnished, with modern kitchens, private

bathrooms, and outdoor seating areas that overlook the fjord. Some cottages even have fireplaces for those chilly evenings.
- Ambiance: Peaceful, with unobstructed views of the fjord and surrounding waterfalls.

What to Do Nearby
- Fjord Cruises: Sail past the Seven Sisters and Suitor waterfalls on a guided boat tour.
- Hike to Skageflå: This historic mountain farm offers breathtaking views of the fjord.
- Drive the Eagle Road: A winding mountain road with hairpin turns and unforgettable viewpoints.

What I Observed
From the cottage's deck, I watched as the light shifted across the fjord, painting the water in shades of blue and green. The sound of cascading waterfalls echoed through the valley. One evening, I spotted a porpoise surfacing in the fjord—a fleeting but magical moment that made me feel deeply connected to this incredible place.

3. Lofoten Cottages (Lofoten Islands)
Location
Nestled on the shores of the Lofoten Islands, these cottages are perfect for those seeking a true Arctic escape. Surrounded by jagged peaks and turquoise waters, they feel wonderfully remote yet incredibly welcoming.

Getting There
- By Plane: Fly into Leknes or Svolvær airports, both of which are short drives from the cottages.
- By Ferry: Accessible by ferry from Bodø to Moskenes, followed by a scenic drive.

What to Expect
- Prices: €150–€300 per night, depending on the cottage's location and amenities.
- Features: Traditional red fishing cabins (rorbuer) with modern interiors, full kitchens, and outdoor seating areas. Many cottages are perched right on the water.
- Ambiance: Rustic charm meets Arctic wonder.

What to Do Nearby
- Kayaking: Paddle through crystal-clear waters surrounded by dramatic peaks.
- Northern Lights: In winter, watch the aurora borealis dance across the night sky.
- Fishing: Join a local fishing expedition to experience Lofoten's maritime heritage.

What I Observed
The first morning in my Lofoten cottage, I stepped out onto the deck to find the water so still it perfectly mirrored the surrounding mountains. The air was crisp, carrying the faint scent of the sea. As I watched fishing boats head out for the day, I felt a deep sense of tranquility, as though the world had slowed just for me.

4. Neset Camping (Byglandsfjord, Southern Norway)

Location

Situated on the shores of Byglandsfjord in Southern Norway, Neset Camping offers cozy cabins surrounded by forest and water.

Getting There
- By Car: A 1.5-hour drive from Kristiansand or a 4.5-hour drive from Oslo.
- By Bus: Buses run from nearby towns to Byglandsfjord.

What to Expect
- Prices: €70–€150 per night, making it one of the most budget-friendly options.
- Features: Compact, well-equipped cabins with kitchens, private bathrooms, and outdoor seating areas. Some cabins are right on the fjord's edge.
- Ambiance: Family-friendly and close to nature.

What to Do Nearby
- Boat Tours: Explore Byglandsfjord on a traditional steamboat, the Bjoren.
- Hiking: Trails in the surrounding forest lead to stunning viewpoints.
- Swimming and Fishing: The fjord's calm waters are perfect for a refreshing dip or fishing.

What I Observed

Evenings at Neset Camping were magical. Families gathered around fire pits, their laughter mingling with the sound of lapping water. One evening, as the sun set behind the forested hills, the fjord turned a deep shade of gold. I sat by the water with my journal, feeling utterly at peace.

Farm Stays: Immersive rural experiences with local charm.

1. Aga Fjord Farm (Hardangerfjord)

Location

Nestled in the heart of Hardangerfjord, Aga Fjord Farm is a historic orchard farm renowned for its breathtaking views and centuries-old cider-making traditions.

Getting There
- By Car: A scenic 2.5-hour drive from Bergen, following the Hardanger National Tourist Route along the fjord's edge.
- By Public Transport: Take a train from Bergen to Voss, then a bus to Aga.

What to Expect
- Prices: €100–€200 per night, depending on the season and room type.
- Accommodations: Stay in beautifully restored farmhouses with traditional wooden interiors and modern comforts.

Each room offers panoramic views of the fjord and surrounding orchards.
- Ambiance: Quiet, serene, and steeped in history.

What to Do on the Farm
- Cider Tasting: Learn about Hardanger's renowned cider production, sample different varieties, and tour the orchards where the apples are grown. (€30–€50 per person).
- Orchard Walks: Wander through apple, pear, and cherry orchards while taking in views of the fjord.
- Farm-to-Table Meals: Enjoy homemade dishes featuring farm-fresh ingredients, from locally smoked trout to apple-based desserts.

What I Observed

As I sat under a blooming apple tree, sipping a glass of crisp cider, the world felt impossibly peaceful. The orchard buzzed with life—bees flitting between blossoms, the occasional cluck of a hen, and the gentle rustle of leaves in the breeze. Later, during a tour of the cidery, I marveled at the dedication of the farmers, who spoke of their craft with pride and passion. It was a moment of pure connection to the land and its people.

2. Skageflå Farm (Geirangerfjord)

Location

High above Geirangerfjord, Skageflå Farm is an abandoned mountain farm that now serves as a unique destination for hikers and history enthusiasts. While no longer operational as a working farm, its remnants and dramatic location offer an unforgettable glimpse into the resilience of Norway's farming heritage.

Getting There
- By Boat and Hike: Take a ferry from Geiranger to the trailhead, then embark on a 2-hour hike up steep but rewarding paths.
- By Car and Hike: Drive to Geiranger and follow signs to hiking trails leading to Skageflå.

What to Expect
- Prices: There's no cost to visit the farm, though guided tours (€50–€100) provide rich historical context.
- Ambiance: Rustic, dramatic, and awe-inspiring. The views from Skageflå are among the most iconic in Norway, with the fjord stretching out below and the Seven Sisters waterfall cascading in the distance.

What to Do on the Farm
- Explore the Ruins: Wander through the old stone walls and learn about the families who farmed this rugged land.
- Photography: Capture the stunning vistas that make Skageflå one of the most photographed spots in Geirangerfjord.
- Reflect: Take a moment to sit on the cliffs and imagine what life was like for the farmers who called this place home.

What I Observed

The hike to Skageflå was challenging but rewarding. As I climbed, I couldn't help but wonder how anyone had lived and worked in such a remote, precarious location. When I reached the top, the view stole my breath. The fjord shimmered below, and the wind carried the faint roar of waterfalls. It was humbling to stand in a place so steeped in history and natural beauty.

3. Herdalssetra (Norddal, Sunnmøre Alps)
Location
Herdalssetra is a summer mountain farm located in the Sunnmøre Alps, where traditional farming practices have been preserved for over 300 years. It's a working farm during the summer months, complete with grazing goats, cows, and sheep.

Getting There
- By Car: A 2-hour drive from Ålesund, following the scenic Trollstigen mountain road.
- By Bus and Hike: Buses run from Ålesund to Norddal, followed by a short hike to the farm.

What to Expect
- Prices: Day visits cost €10–€20, which include a guided tour and tasting. Overnight stays in rustic cabins are priced at €70–€120.
- Ambiance: Lively, with the sounds of animals and the laughter of farmers filling the air.

What to Do on the Farm
- Milk Goats: Try your hand at goat milking and learn about the process of making traditional cheese.
- Taste Farm Products: Sample goat cheese, fresh milk, and other homemade treats.
- Explore the Surroundings: Hike the nearby trails, which offer sweeping views of the Sunnmøre Alps.

What I Observed
Herdalssetra felt alive in a way few places do. The goats trotted happily through the meadows, their bells chiming in harmony with the babbling brook nearby. I tried goat milking for the first time—a surprisingly tricky endeavor—and felt a deep appreciation for the work of the farmers. Later, as I nibbled on creamy goat cheese and fresh bread, I marveled at how the simplest foods can taste so extraordinary when made with love and care.

4. Undredal Stølsysteri (Undredal)
Location
Nestled along Aurlandsfjord, Undredal is a tiny village famous for its goat cheese and traditional stave church.

Getting There
- By Car: A 20-minute drive from Flåm, following the fjord's edge.
- By Ferry: Undredal is a stop on the ferry route between Flåm and Gudvangen.

What to Expect
- Prices: €50–€70 for a guided tour and cheese tasting.
- Ambiance: Intimate, with a strong sense of community.

What to Do on the Farm
- Learn About Cheese-Making: Tour the dairy and watch the process of making

Norway's famous brown goat cheese (geitost).
- Taste the Cheese: Try a variety of goat cheeses, from creamy and mild to bold and caramelized.
- Visit the Stave Church: Explore Norway's smallest stave church, built in the 12th century.

What I Observed

Undredal was a feast for the senses. The aroma of cheese filled the air as I stepped into the tiny dairy, where copper kettles bubbled with rich goat's milk. The cheese tasting was an adventure in itself—each bite revealed new layers of flavor, from sweet to tangy to nutty. As I wandered through the village afterward, the warmth of the locals made me feel like part of their story.

Cruise Ship Cabins: Uninterrupted Fjord Views from the Water

Cruise ships catering to the Norwegian fjords offer a range of cabin types to suit every traveler. Each option enhances your experience in its own way, depending on your preferences.

1. Oceanview Cabins
Features: A large picture window or porthole framing the views of the fjords. Perfect for travelers who want stunning sights without stepping outside their cabin.
What I Observed: On one quiet evening, I sat on the window ledge, watching the setting sun bathe the cliffs in hues of amber and rose. The reflection on the water was so mesmerizing, I forgot I was indoors.
Price Range: €150–€300 per night.

2. Balcony Cabins
Features: Private balconies with outdoor seating, offering uninterrupted views and fresh air. There's nothing like starting your day with a cup of coffee on your own deck, surrounded by nature.
What to Observe: Look for seals lounging on rocks, porpoises playing in the water, and birds soaring past the cliffs.
Price Range: €300–€600 per night.

3. Suites
Features: Larger spaces with luxurious amenities, including separate living areas and larger balconies. Some even come with butler service.
Why You'll Love It: Suites elevate your journey with unmatched comfort and exclusivity. Imagine soaking in a private hot tub while gazing at the fjords.
Price Range: €600–€1,200 per night.

What to Do in Your Cabin

- Enjoy the Silence: Fjords are known for their profound stillness. Open your window or step onto your balcony to listen to the gentle sound of water lapping against the ship.

- **Stargazing:** In winter, watch for the Northern Lights from the comfort of your room. In summer, the Midnight Sun casts a soft, golden glow over the landscape.
- **Photography:** Use your vantage point to capture unique angles of the fjords. The way the light dances on the water is a photographer's dream.

What to Expect
- **Comfort:** Modern cruise ship cabins are equipped with plush beds, ample storage, and en-suite bathrooms. Expect clean, cozy interiors that complement the natural surroundings.
- **Personalized Service:** Attentive crew members ensure your stay is as seamless as possible, from room service to arranging special requests.
- **Proximity to Nature:** Unlike traditional accommodations, cruise ship cabins offer ever-changing views, bringing the fjords directly to your doorstep.

Airbnb and Vacation Rentals: Unique and Flexible Options for Personalized Stays

1. Modern Apartment in Bergen
Location
Located near the historic Bryggen Wharf, this sleek apartment offers the perfect mix of city charm and fjord access.

Getting There
- **By Car:** A 20-minute drive from Bergen Airport.
- **By Public Transport:** Take the light rail to the city center; the apartment is a 10-minute walk from the stop.

What to Expect
- **Prices:** €100–€180 per night.
- **Features:** Spacious one-bedroom apartment with a fully equipped kitchen, stylish decor, and large windows that flood the space with light.
- **Ambiance:** Modern and urban, with touches of Scandinavian design.

What to Do Nearby
- **Explore Bryggen:** Wander through the colorful wooden buildings and learn about Bergen's Hanseatic past.
- **Visit the Fish Market:** Sample fresh seafood or pick up ingredients for a home-cooked meal.
- **Ride the Fløibanen Funicular:** Ascend Mount Fløyen for panoramic views.

What I Observed
The apartment felt like a true oasis after a day of exploring. The open-plan living room was perfect for relaxing with a glass of wine, while the kitchen made it easy to whip up a quick meal with ingredients I'd picked up from the market. Looking out at the city lights

twinkling against the backdrop of the mountains, I felt perfectly at home.

2. Seaside Cabin in Lofoten
Location
Situated on the shores of the Lofoten Islands, this charming cabin offers direct access to some of Norway's most dramatic scenery.

Getting There
- By Plane: Fly into Leknes Airport, followed by a 30-minute drive to the cabin.
- By Ferry: Take a ferry from Bodø to Moskenes, then drive to the cabin.

What to Expect
- Prices: €150–€300 per night.
- Features: Traditional red fishing cabin (rorbuer) with modern amenities, including a fully equipped kitchen and a terrace overlooking the water.
- Ambiance: Rustic yet comfortable, with unbeatable proximity to nature.

What to Do Nearby
- Kayaking: Paddle through the clear waters surrounded by jagged peaks.
- Northern Lights Watching: In winter, the cabin offers a prime spot for viewing the aurora borealis.
- Hiking: Explore trails leading to scenic viewpoints.

What I Observed
Staying in this cabin felt like a dream. Each morning, I stepped outside to the sound of waves gently lapping against the dock. The air was crisp, carrying the faint scent of salt and seaweed. Evenings were spent curled up by the fire, gazing out at the stars through large windows. It was the perfect blend of adventure and tranquility.

3. Historic Home in Aurland
Location
Perched above Aurlandsfjord, this historic home combines traditional Norwegian architecture with breathtaking views.

Getting There
- By Car: A 2.5-hour drive from Bergen via the scenic E16.
- By Public Transport: Buses connect Aurland to nearby towns like Flåm.

What to Expect
- Prices: €120–€200 per night.
- Features: A charming wooden house with two bedrooms, a fireplace, and a garden overlooking the fjord.
- Ambiance: Cozy and nostalgic, with authentic touches like hand-carved furniture.

What to Do Nearby
- Explore Stegastein Viewpoint: Just a short drive away, this platform offers panoramic views of the fjord.
- Visit Undredal: A quaint village famous for its goat cheese and stave church.
- Take a Fjord Cruise: Experience the beauty of Aurlandsfjord and Nærøyfjord from the water.

What I Observed
The house felt like stepping back in time, yet it had all the modern comforts I needed. The view from the garden was nothing short of

spectacular—fjords stretching as far as the eye could see, framed by snow-capped peaks. Watching the sunset from the porch, wrapped in a warm blanket, was a moment I'll never forget.

Why You Should Try These Stays

both cruise ship cabins and vacation rentals offer experiences that go beyond accommodation. They become part of your story, enhancing your journey in unique ways.

- Cruise Ship Cabins: For those who want to feel the constant embrace of the fjords, these cabins offer unparalleled access to Norway's natural wonders.
- Airbnb and Vacation Rentals: Perfect for travelers seeking flexibility and a personal touch, these homes allow you to live like a local while immersing yourself in the beauty of your surroundings.

Chapter 10: Sustainability and Responsible Travel

Reducing your environmental impact as a traveler

Travel has the power to inspire, educate, and connect us with the beauty of the world. However, it also comes with an environmental cost—carbon emissions, waste generation, and the strain on local resources can leave a lasting footprint on the places we cherish most. The good news? With a few thoughtful changes, we can travel more responsibly, ensuring that our adventures not only enrich our lives but also protect the planet for future generations.

1. Choose Sustainable Modes of Transportation

Transportation is one of the largest contributors to a traveler's carbon footprint. By selecting greener options, you can significantly reduce your impact.

Fly Smarter
- Opt for Direct Flights: Takeoffs and landings generate the most emissions, so choosing non-stop flights minimizes your carbon footprint.
- Offset Your Carbon: Many airlines offer carbon offset programs, allowing you to support renewable energy or reforestation projects to balance your emissions.
- Fly Economy: More passengers per flight means a lower per-person footprint.

Embrace Trains, Buses, and Ferries
Overland transportation like trains and buses produces far fewer emissions compared to flying.
Tip: In regions like Europe, trains not only reduce your impact but also allow you to enjoy stunning scenery along the way.

What I Experienced
During a trip to Norway, I took the Flåm Railway instead of flying between cities. Watching waterfalls cascade down cliffs and passing through mountain valleys was infinitely more rewarding than staring at the seatback screen on a plane.

2. Pack Light and Smart
The heavier the load, the more fuel is required to transport it, whether by plane, car, or bus. Packing light not only reduces emissions but also makes your trip easier to manage.

What to Do
- Pack Versatile Clothing: Choose items that can be layered and reused in multiple ways.
- Use Eco-Friendly Products: Switch to solid shampoo bars, refillable toiletry containers, and biodegradable sunscreens to reduce plastic waste.
- Avoid Overpacking: Bring only what you truly need. Excess luggage consumes more energy during transit.

Pro Tip
Invest in a high-quality, durable travel bag that will last for years, reducing the waste of constantly replacing luggage.

3. Support Sustainable Accommodations
Where you stay can have a huge impact on your environmental footprint. Fortunately, many accommodations are adopting greener practices.

What to Look For
- Green Certifications: Choose hotels or lodges certified by organizations like Green Key, EarthCheck, or LEED. These certifications indicate eco-friendly operations, from energy efficiency to waste reduction.
- Locally Owned Accommodations: Staying in family-run inns, guesthouses, or Airbnbs supports the local economy and often has a smaller environmental impact than large hotel chains.
- Eco-Lodges: These properties are designed to blend harmoniously with their surroundings and prioritize sustainability.

My Experience
While exploring the fjords, I stayed in an eco-lodge that powered itself entirely with solar energy. Walking into my room, the warm glow of natural wood and panoramic windows overlooking the fjord made it clear that sustainability and comfort can go hand in hand.

4. Respect Local Ecosystems
From hiking trails to coral reefs, natural habitats are a major draw for travelers. Protecting these delicate ecosystems ensures they can be enjoyed for generations to come.

What to Do

- Stay on Marked Trails: Veering off trails can harm plant life and disturb wildlife habitats.
- Avoid Single-Use Plastics: Carry a reusable water bottle, utensils, and tote bags to reduce waste.
- Say No to Wildlife Exploitation: Avoid attractions that exploit animals, such as elephant rides or swimming with captive dolphins. Instead, support ethical wildlife tours that prioritize conservation.

What I Observed
Hiking through Norway's pristine landscapes, I noticed how well-marked trails and respectful hikers preserved the untouched beauty of the area. It reminded me that we are guests in these wild places, with a responsibility to leave them as we found them.

5. Eat Local, Eat Smart
Food is a delicious part of any journey, but it's also an opportunity to make environmentally conscious choices.

What to Do
- Choose Local and Seasonal Foods: Reducing the distance food travels lowers its carbon footprint. Plus, you'll enjoy fresher, tastier dishes.
- Eat Less Meat: Livestock farming is a major contributor to greenhouse gas emissions. Consider trying vegetarian or plant-based options while traveling.
- Bring Your Own Containers: For takeout meals or snacks, reusable containers help reduce single-use packaging.

My Experience
In Tromsø, I dined on Arctic char sourced from a nearby fjord. The simplicity and freshness of the meal made it unforgettable, and knowing it was sustainably caught added to my appreciation.

6. Minimize Energy and Water Use
Even small changes to your daily habits can reduce resource consumption during your stay.

What to Do
- Reuse Towels and Linens: Request that your towels and bed linens aren't washed daily to save water and energy.
- Turn Off Electronics: When leaving your room, switch off lights, unplug chargers, and adjust the thermostat to conserve energy.
- Take Shorter Showers: Every drop counts, especially in regions where water is scarce.

Pro Tip
Many accommodations now display signs encouraging eco-friendly practices—be sure to follow these guidelines to help lighten your impact.

7. Travel Off the Beaten Path
Mass tourism can strain popular destinations, leading to overcrowding and resource depletion. By visiting lesser-known locations, you not only reduce pressure on overtouristed spots but also discover unique, unspoiled experiences.

What to Do
- Research Alternatives: Instead of heading straight to Paris, why not

explore the stunning countryside of Dordogne? Swap Venice for the enchanting canals of Annecy.
- Travel During Off-Peak Seasons: Visit popular destinations in the shoulder or low seasons to reduce your footprint and enjoy a quieter experience.

Important Tip
Always be mindful of how your presence affects local communities, ensuring that your visit benefits them rather than burdens them.

8. Offset Your Carbon Emissions
Even with the best intentions, some environmental impact is unavoidable. Carbon offset programs allow you to balance your emissions by supporting sustainable initiatives.

What to Look For
- Verified Projects: Choose offset programs certified by organizations like Gold Standard or Verified Carbon Standard. These programs fund efforts like reforestation, renewable energy, and methane capture.
- Transparency: Reputable programs clearly outline how funds are used and the impact they've achieved.

What I Experienced
Before a long-haul flight, I contributed to a carbon offset project that planted trees in deforested areas. Knowing my trip was helping to restore ecosystems made the journey feel even more purposeful.

Supporting local communities and economies

Travel isn't just about discovering new places—it's also about fostering connections with the people who call those places home. Supporting local communities and economies is one of the most meaningful ways to give back as a traveler. By choosing to engage with local businesses, artisans, and initiatives, we ensure that tourism becomes a force for good, directly benefiting the communities we visit while preserving their unique cultures, traditions, and environments.

1. Choose Locally Owned Accommodations
Staying at locally owned lodgings—whether it's family-run guesthouses, boutique hotels, or eco-lodges—not only provides a more

authentic experience but also ensures that your money remains within the local community.

What to Do
- Look for Family-Run Guesthouses: These often offer a more personal experience, with hosts eager to share stories and insider tips about their hometown.
- Support Eco-Lodges: Many eco-lodges prioritize sustainability and hire local staff, creating employment opportunities for the surrounding community.
- Avoid Large International Chains: While convenient, these often funnel profits out of the local economy.

What I Experienced
In Aurland, Norway, I stayed at a charming fjord-side guesthouse run by a local family. Each morning, the host prepared a breakfast featuring cheeses and jams from nearby farms. They even offered to guide me to their favorite hiking trails—insights you'd never get from a big chain hotel. Every moment felt personal and rooted in the community.

2. Eat and Shop Local
Dining at locally owned restaurants and shopping for handmade goods are among the easiest ways to directly support communities while immersing yourself in their culture.

What to Do
- Dine at Local Restaurants: Seek out small, family-run eateries rather than international chains. These often serve traditional dishes made from locally sourced ingredients.
- Visit Farmers' Markets: Farmers' markets are treasures of local produce, homemade goodies, and a chance to meet the people behind your food.
- Buy Handmade Crafts: Invest in unique, locally crafted items like pottery, textiles, or jewelry. These purchases support artisans and preserve traditional skills.

Tips for Shopping Ethically
Ask Questions: Enquire about the origin of the product to ensure it's genuinely local.
Avoid Mass-Produced Souvenirs: Instead, look for unique items that reflect the community's traditions.

What I Observed
While wandering a market in Tromsø, I came across an artisan crafting jewelry from Arctic driftwood. Each piece told a story of its journey through icy waters, and buying a necklace felt like carrying a piece of the Arctic home with me. The artisan's face lit up as we chatted—it was clear how much heart went into their craft.

3. Participate in Responsible Tours and Experiences

Engaging in local tours and experiences led by residents is not only enriching but also ensures your tourism dollars go directly to the community.

What to Do
- Hire Local Guides: Seek out guides who are knowledgeable and live in the area—they'll often have the best stories and hidden gems to share.

- Join Workshops or Classes: Learn a traditional skill, like weaving, pottery, or cooking. These experiences give back to the community while deepening your cultural understanding.
- Support Wildlife Conservation Efforts: Choose tours that respect wildlife and contribute to habitat preservation.

What I Experienced
In a small village near Hardangerfjord, I joined a cider-making workshop. The farmer who led the session shared tales of how his family had been crafting cider for generations, and every sip of the finished product felt like a celebration of his heritage. The small fee I paid directly supported his farm—a win-win.

4. Respect Local Customs and Traditions
Part of supporting communities is showing respect for their way of life. Tourism should celebrate and uplift cultures, not disrupt or exploit them.

What to Do
- Learn Basic Phrases: A simple "hello" or "thank you" in the local language goes a long way in showing respect.
- Dress Modestly: Be mindful of local customs regarding attire, especially in conservative areas.
- Follow Cultural Norms: Respect rituals, sacred spaces, and traditions, even if they differ from your own.

Why It Matters
When you respect a community's culture, you build bridges of trust and mutual appreciation. This strengthens the positive impact of tourism and fosters long-term relationships between visitors and locals.

5. Reduce Your Environmental Impact
Sustainable tourism is integral to supporting communities, as environmental degradation often disproportionately affects local populations.

What to Do
- Minimize Plastic Waste: Carry a reusable water bottle, utensils, and bags to reduce single-use plastics.
- Avoid Overcrowded Destinations: Spread your tourism dollars to lesser-known locations, reducing pressure on heavily trafficked areas.
- Use Local Transport: Public buses, trains, and bike rentals not only lower your carbon footprint but also contribute to the local economy.

What I Observed
In Norway, many small communities take pride in their pristine natural surroundings. Respecting these environments—by staying on marked trails and leaving no trace—felt like a way of honoring the people who call them home.

6. Donate Responsibly
If you feel inspired to contribute financially, make sure your donations are impactful and ethical.

What to Do
- Support Community Projects: Look for reputable local charities or grassroots organizations that work directly with residents.

- Avoid Giving to Beggars: While well-intentioned, direct handouts can perpetuate dependency. Instead, support organizations that provide sustainable solutions.
- Volunteer Thoughtfully: If offering your time, ensure the program genuinely benefits the community and aligns with your skills.

Important Tip

Do your research before donating to ensure your contribution is being used effectively. Websites like Charity Navigator or GuideStar can help verify organizations' legitimacy.

Chapter 11: Practical Travel Tips

Navigating Norwegian culture and etiquette

As someone who's had the privilege of exploring this magnificent country, I quickly realized that navigating Norwegian culture is about appreciating its subtlety and depth. Norwegians value simplicity, equality, and a quiet pride in their way of life. Let me guide you through the essential aspects of Norwegian culture and etiquette, so you can not only blend in seamlessly but also build meaningful connections with the locals.

1. The Value of Equality and "Janteloven"

At the heart of Norwegian culture is the principle of equality, often encapsulated by "Janteloven," or the Law of Jante. This social code emphasizes modesty, humility, and the importance of not elevating oneself above others.

What This Means for You
- Be Humble: Avoid bragging or displaying wealth and accomplishments. Norwegians appreciate modesty and down-to-earth behavior.
- Respect Equality: Treat everyone with equal respect, regardless of their profession or social status. Hierarchies are less pronounced in Norway.

My Experience

While chatting with a local fisherman in Lofoten, I was struck by his humility despite his impressive knowledge of Arctic waters. His unassuming nature made our conversation all the more genuine and heartfelt.

2. Punctuality: A Sign of Respect
Time is valued in Norway, and punctuality is seen as a sign of respect for others. Whether you're meeting someone for coffee or catching a tour, it's important to be on time.

What This Means for You
- Arrive Promptly: Being late, even by a few minutes, can come across as disrespectful.
- Plan Ahead: Account for weather conditions or transportation delays, especially in rural areas.

What I Observed
When I arrived exactly at 7:00 PM for a dinner invitation, my host smiled and said, "You're Norwegian now!" Punctuality isn't just about time—it's about thoughtfulness.

3. Personal Space and Privacy

Norwegians value personal space and privacy. They may come across as reserved or distant at first, but this is not out of rudeness—it's simply part of their cultural norm.

What This Means for You
- Respect Physical Space: Avoid standing too close to others in queues or public spaces.
- Wait for the Right Moment: Norwegians may not initiate conversation with strangers, but they are warm and engaging once the interaction begins.

Important Tip
Don't mistake quietness for disinterest—Norwegians often prefer meaningful discussions over small talk.

4. Nature Is Sacred
Norwegians are deeply connected to nature, and outdoor activities are an integral part of their lifestyle. The concept of "friluftsliv," or open-air living, reflects their love for the outdoors.

What This Means for You
- Embrace the Outdoors: Take part in hiking, skiing, or simply enjoying a walk through the woods. It's a way to connect with both nature and the Norwegian spirit.
- Respect the Environment: Leave no trace when exploring. Norwegians take environmental stewardship seriously.

My Experience
Hiking in Jotunheimen National Park, I encountered locals who greeted me with warm smiles despite the remote trails. I realized that being in nature is a shared joy in Norway—something cherished by all.

5. Dining Etiquette: Keep It Simple
Norwegian dining habits reflect their love for simplicity and quality. Meals are often relaxed but come with unspoken rules of politeness.

What This Means for You

Wait Before Eating: Don't begin eating until your host says, "Velbekomme" (Enjoy your meal).

Bring a Gift: If invited to someone's home, bring a small gift like flowers, wine, or chocolates.

Offer to Split the Bill: When dining out, it's common to pay your share unless the host explicitly offers to cover it.

What I Observed
When invited to a local family's home for dinner, I was touched by their hospitality. We enjoyed a traditional meal of rakfisk (fermented fish), and they appreciated the small bottle of wine I brought as a token of gratitude.

6. Communication: Direct and Respectful
Norwegians tend to communicate directly and honestly. They appreciate straightforwardness over embellishments.

What This Means for You
Be Honest: Say what you mean and mean what you say. Norwegians value sincerity.

Use a Polite Tone: While direct, it's important to remain respectful and avoid being overly blunt.

Pro Tip
Address people by their first names, as Norwegian society is generally informal. Titles are rarely used, even in professional settings.

7. Sustainability Is a Way of Life
Norwegians are leaders in sustainable living, and this mindset extends to every aspect of their culture.

What This Means for You
- Recycle and Reuse: Follow local recycling practices and use reusable bags or bottles.
- Support Local: Choose locally sourced products and businesses to contribute positively to the community.
- Use Public Transport: Norway's efficient public transportation system is not only convenient but also eco-friendly.

My Experience
In Oslo, I noticed how seamlessly sustainability was integrated into daily life—from electric buses to organic food markets. Even as a visitor, I felt inspired to adopt these practices.

8. Embracing Silence and Tranquility
Silence is not awkward in Norwegian culture—it's often seen as a natural and comfortable state, especially in social settings or during meals.

What This Means for You
- Don't Feel Pressured to Fill Silences: Enjoy the calm and use the moment for reflection.
- Be Mindful in Nature: Norwegians often seek solitude in the outdoors, so respect the quiet atmosphere on trails or in national parks.

Currency and language basics

Currency in Norway: The Norwegian Krone (NOK)
Norway's official currency is the Norwegian Krone, often abbreviated as NOK or simply referred to as "kr." The krone means "crown,"

and it's a stable currency that's widely accepted across the country.

Basic Facts About the Norwegian Krone
- **Coins:** Coins come in denominations of 1, 5, 10, and 20 kroner. These are commonly used for small purchases or tips.
- **Banknotes:** Banknotes are available in 50, 100, 200, 500, and 1,000 kroner. Modern, sleek designs reflect Norway's rich heritage and nature.
- **Currency Symbol:** While NOK is the international abbreviation, you might also see prices written with "kr"—e.g., "50 kr" for 50 kroner.

What You Should Know
- **Exchange Rates:** The exchange rate fluctuates but generally hovers around 1 USD = 10–11 NOK and 1 Euro = 11–12 NOK. Check rates before you travel for accurate conversions.
- **Cash or Card?** Norway is largely cashless, with credit and debit cards accepted nearly everywhere, including taxis, grocery stores, and even rural locations. Cards with a chip and PIN are recommended.
- **Contactless Payments:** Mobile payment systems like Apple Pay or Google Pay are widely accepted, making transactions effortless.

Practical Tips for Using Currency
1. Withdraw Locally: If you need cash, withdraw NOK from local ATMs (called "Minibanks") to avoid high exchange fees.
2. Skip the Cash Exchange: Currency exchange services often charge high rates. Using ATMs directly is more economical.
3. Ask for Receipts: Tax refunds are available for some purchases over 315 NOK. Keep your receipts for potential reimbursement at the airport.

My Experience
In Oslo, I rarely needed cash. Even at outdoor markets and food stalls, vendors happily accepted contactless payments. When I traveled to smaller villages, I carried just a small amount of cash for emergencies—but even then, my debit card sufficed most of the time.

Language in Norway: Norwegian and Beyond

The official language of Norway is Norwegian (Norsk), a North Germanic language with two written forms: Bokmål and Nynorsk. While Norwegian is spoken by nearly all Norwegians, you'll also find that English is widely understood and spoken, particularly in urban and tourist-friendly areas.

Quick Norwegian Language Overview
1. Two Written Forms:
Bokmål (literally "Book Language") is the most widely used form and is what you'll typically see on signs, menus, and official communications.
Nynorsk ("New Norwegian") is derived from rural dialects and is used in certain regions and schools.

2. Sami Language: In Northern Norway, the Sami people speak their own distinct language alongside Norwegian. This Indigenous language is an integral part of Sami culture.

What to Observe About the Language
- Politeness: Norwegians are generally reserved and polite. Using "takk" (thank you) and "vær så snill" (please) will always be appreciated.
- Pronunciation: Norwegian is melodic and gentle. Don't be afraid to try—even if your accent isn't perfect, locals will admire your effort.

Practical Tips for Language
1. **Start Small**: Focus on learning key phrases rather than attempting full sentences, especially if you're a beginner.
2. **Use Apps:** Download language apps like Duolingo or Google Translate to help with pronunciation and on-the-go translations.
3. **Embrace English**: If you're unsure, most Norwegians will happily switch to English without hesitation.

My Experience
While dining in Tromsø, I made an effort to thank my server in Norwegian: "Tusen takk!" Her warm smile and cheerful "Bare hyggelig!" (You're welcome) reminded me how small gestures can create connections.

Emergency contacts and safety tips

1. Emergency Contacts in Norway

Norway has a well-organized emergency response system. Here are the key numbers you should memorize or save on your phone:

Universal Emergency Number: 112
Use 112 to contact the police, ambulance, or fire department in any emergency. Operators speak English and can direct your call appropriately.

Direct Emergency Numbers
- Police: 112 (for reporting crimes or safety concerns).
- Ambulance: 113 (for medical emergencies).
- Fire Department: 110 (for fires or hazardous incidents).

Additional Contacts
- Medical Information Helpline (non-emergencies): 116 117
- For non-critical medical situations, such as minor injuries or illnesses, this number connects you to healthcare professionals.
- Tourist Information Emergency Assistance: Many tourist offices can provide guidance in less critical situations. The Visit Norway website or local tourism centers can also help direct you.
- Poison Control: 22 59 13 00

2. Safety Tips for Travelers in Norway
While Norway is ranked as one of the safest countries in the world, it's always wise to stay prepared and informed. Here are essential safety tips to keep in mind:

General Safety
- Low Crime Rate: Norway's crime rate is very low, but petty theft, such as pickpocketing, can occur in

tourist-heavy areas. Always keep an eye on your belongings.
- **Secure Valuables:** Use a money belt or keep your valuables in a secure, hidden place. Avoid flaunting expensive items.
- **Be Aware of Surroundings:** Stay vigilant in crowded areas, such as public transport hubs and markets.

Navigating Nature Safely

Norway's wild and stunning landscapes demand both respect and preparation.

1. Hiking Tips:
- **Stick to Marked Trails:** Norway's trails are well-marked, but venturing off-path can be dangerous and harmful to the environment.
- **Check the Weather:** Weather in Norway can be unpredictable, especially in mountainous or coastal areas. Check forecasts before heading out.
- **Carry Essentials:** Bring a map, compass, water, snacks, a first-aid kit, and layers of clothing for hikes. Even in summer, temperatures can drop quickly.

2. Be Cautious Around Water:
- Fjords and waterfalls are stunning but can be slippery and dangerous. Avoid standing too close to edges, especially in wet weather.
- For kayaking or boat tours, always wear a life jacket.

3. Winter Safety:
- **Ice and Snow:** Be cautious when walking in winter. Use crampons or ice grips on icy trails or streets.
- **Avalanche Risks:** In winter, some mountainous areas are prone to avalanches. Always check local warnings and stay in designated skiing or hiking areas.

4. Wildlife:
- Moose, reindeer, and sheep are common on rural roads. Drive slowly, especially at dawn and dusk, to avoid collisions.
- Observe wildlife from a distance—do not approach or feed animals.

3. Healthcare and First Aid

Norway's healthcare system is world-class, and visitors have access to emergency medical services if needed.

What to Know
- **European Health Insurance Card (EHIC):** If you're an EU/EEA citizen, carry an EHIC card for free or reduced-cost medical care.
- **Travel Insurance:** Comprehensive travel insurance is essential. Ensure your policy covers medical emergencies, outdoor activities, and any pre-existing conditions.
- **Pharmacies (Apotek):** Most towns have a pharmacy where you can purchase over-the-counter medication. Look for signs that say "Apotek." Some pharmacies in larger cities have extended hours.

First Aid Kits

If you're planning outdoor adventures, carry a first aid kit with bandages, antiseptics, pain relievers, and blister pads. These can be lifesavers during long hikes.

4. Transportation and Road Safety

Norway's public transport system is reliable and safe, but driving in certain areas can pose unique challenges.

Public Transport
- Buses and Trains: Public transport is punctual and well-organized. Be mindful of schedules, especially in rural areas where services may be less frequent.
- Taxis: Registered taxis are safe, but they can be expensive. Ridesharing apps like Bolt are sometimes available in larger cities.

Driving Tips
- Winter Roads: Winter conditions can make driving challenging. Rent a car with winter tires and be prepared for icy roads.
- Watch for Wildlife: Animals frequently cross rural roads, so always drive cautiously.
- Obey Speed Limits: Norway has strict traffic laws, and speeding fines are substantial.

5. Emergency Apps and Resources

For added security and peace of mind, download these apps to your phone before traveling:

- 112 App: Norway's emergency app allows you to send your location to emergency services with one click.
- YR Weather App: Provides accurate weather forecasts, crucial for outdoor activities.
- Red Cross First Aid App: A valuable guide for managing first aid situations in remote areas.

6. Be Prepared for Communication Challenges

Although English is widely spoken in Norway, having basic Norwegian phrases on hand can be helpful in emergencies. Keep a list of emergency-related phrases, like:

- Help! – Hjelp!
- I need a doctor. – Jeg trenger en lege.
- Where is the nearest hospital? – Hvor er nærmeste sykehus?
- Call the police. – Ring politiet.

Having these phrases written down or saved in your phone ensures you're ready for any situation.

7. Know the Local Laws

Familiarize yourself with some basic laws to avoid unwittingly landing in trouble:

Alcohol Rules: Drinking alcohol in public spaces is generally prohibited. Alcohol is sold only in licensed stores, and buying stronger beverages like spirits is limited to Vinmonopolet stores.

Wild Camping: Norway's "Allemannsretten" (Right to Roam) allows wild camping, but respect the rules by camping at least 150 meters from private homes and avoiding protected areas.

Chapter 12: The Journey's End

Conclusion: A Journey Worth Taking

As we conclude this exploration of Norway—the Land of the Midnight Sun and Northern Lights—I hope you find yourself not only enchanted by its fjords, mountains, and auroras but also inspired by its people, culture, and sustainable way of life. Traveling to this breathtaking country is not just a journey through its landscapes; it's an invitation to immerse yourself in its very soul. Every hike, meal, or quiet moment by a fjord has the power to leave an imprint on your heart.

Why Norway Matters

Norway isn't just another dot on the map—it's an experience that touches every sense, every emotion, and every corner of your soul. The fjords, with their towering cliffs and still waters, will remind you of the majesty of the natural world. The snowy peaks and shimmering Northern Lights will awaken your sense of wonder. And the culture—a seamless blend of tradition, innovation, and simplicity—will show you the beauty of living thoughtfully and harmoniously.

But beyond what you see and feel is what you can give. As travelers, we have the unique opportunity to connect with local communities, support sustainable practices, and leave a positive mark on the places we visit. When you stand on the edge of Pulpit Rock, or sip cider in a Hardangerfjord orchard, or share a smile with a local artisan in Tromsø, you're not just a visitor—you're part of something bigger.

The Lessons Norway Teaches Us
1. **Live in Harmony with Nature:** Norway's deep respect for its environment is a reminder of the responsibility we share to protect our planet. Whether it's by hiking mindfully, reducing waste, or supporting eco-friendly practices, we all have a role to play.
2. **Value Simplicity:** In a world that often feels rushed and complex, Norway's culture shows us the joy of slowing down, savoring moments, and appreciating the little things—like the first sip of coffee on a snowy morning or the quiet beauty of a mountainside.
3. **Celebrate Connections**: From local farmers to tour guides, the people of Norway have a way of making every encounter meaningful. These connections, however brief, stay with you and enrich your experience.

Parting Thoughts

Norway is a gift—one that gives far more than it takes. It offers inspiration through its landscapes, wisdom through its culture, and peace through its way of life. Whether you find yourself kayaking through serene fjords, watching the aurora dance across a winter sky, or sharing laughter with a Sami guide, you'll carry those moments with you long after your journey ends.

As you prepare for your adventure, I hope you'll travel not just with your luggage but with your heart wide open. Let curiosity guide you, respect ground you, and wonder fill you. Travel to see the beauty of Norway, but more importantly, travel to feel it. And in doing so, you'll discover that the journey matters just as much as the destination.

Thank you for letting me be part of your travel planning. I know that your time in Norway will be extraordinary—and perhaps, life-changing.

Printed in Great Britain
by Amazon